AF685925

Forensic Accounting, Fraud Investigation And Fraud Analytics

ADIL KHAN

Published by ADIL KHAN, 2024.

Also by ADIL KHAN

Business Strategy Understand What It Takes To Be Successful In Business
Emotional Intelligence Gaining Control Over Emotions
Project Management - Complete Guide For A+ Project Managers
Accounting 101 Learn The Basic Principles The Right Way
Influencer Marketing Launch Powerful Campaigns In 10 Steps
Sales Skills Mastery: Sales Story & Metaphor Techniques
Proven Manifestation, Law Of Attraction Self Hypnosis System
Forensic Accounting, Fraud Investigation And Fraud Analytics

Table of Contents

Copyright

Copyright © 2024 by **Adil Khan**. All rights reserved. No part of this book may be reproduced, scanned, or distributed in any printed or electronic form without permission. Please do not participate in or encourage piracy of copyrighted materials in violation of the author's rights. Purchase only authorized editions.

Forensic Accounting, Fraud Investigation And Fraud Analytics

First Edition: Feb 2024

Book Design by **Adil Khan**

About

This comprehensive Book is very helpful to budding professionals and students who have developed a deep passion towards forensic accounting and audit.

Forensic accounting is the investigation of fraud or financial manipulation by performing extremely detailed research and analysis of financial information. Forensic accountants are often hired to prepare for litigation related to insurance claims, insolvency, divorces, embezzlement, fraud, skimming, and any type of financial theft.

A forensic audit is an analysis and review of the financial records of a company or person to extract facts, which can be used in a court of law. Forensic auditing is a speciality in the accounting industry, and most major accounting firms have a department of forensic auditing. Forensic audits include the experience in accounting and auditing practices as well as expert knowledge of forensic audit's legal framework.

Forensic audits cover a large spectrum of investigative activities. There may be a forensic audit to prosecute a party for fraud, embezzlement or other financial crimes. The auditor may be called in during the process of a forensic audit to serve as an expert witness during trial proceedings. Forensic audits could also include situations that do not involve financial fraud, such as bankruptcy filing disputes, closures of businesses, and divorces.

Fundamentals of PCI-DSS

Hello, and welcome to Fundamentals of PCI-DSS Book! In this Book, we are going to cover everything related to this type of industry regulation. Let's take a moment just to cover both the goals and chapters of this Book. Hello, and welcome to the Fundamentals of PCI-DSS Book. In this Book, we have one major goal, which is shedding light on the PCI-DSS framework. And I mean both in general terms - what the PCI-DSS are - the standards - but also the requirements of the framework itself. The 12 Requirements in deep detail. We are going to touch on multiple topics, including: What are the essential terms and keywords used in the PCI-DSS, such as the CDE, or Card Data Environment, or CHD, the Cardholder Data, including SAD, which is the Sensitive Authentication Data.

Don't worry - they may seem intimidating, but they will show up multiple times! Then, what are the 12 requirements of the PCI-DSS, in detail, as well as the sub-requirements of every single one of these! From firewalls, to anti-viruses, to digital and physical access control, strong encryption of data - both in storage and in transit - and many other requirements! Also, a brief history of the PCI-DSS framework, and relevant past versions. Or, how the assessment process itself works, through one of two methods, which are the ROCs, or Reports on Compliance, or the SAQs, or self-assessment questionnaires.

This Book on the fundamentals of PCI-DSS is split into two simple chapters. First, we'll cover the essentials. This will be a short introduction. What are the key terms used? How does the assessment process work? How does a payment itself work? And so on. And then, we'll dive deep into the 12 Requirements, including all types of procedures and policies! We'll cover every single one of the 12 requirements, as well as what each represents. This will be the bulk of the Book, for sure! So, as you see, in this Book, we will have two major chapters. One focused on the essentials, such as the terminology, assessment process, and more. And then, we are going to dive deep into the 12 requirements.

We are now at the Essentials chapter. That is, we are going to cover some basics related to the PCI-DSS. What are some basic terms, what is the assessment process, and more. Let's take a moment, just to review the topics for this chapter. Welcome to the PCI-DSS Essentials chapter, where we will cover the basics of the framework, before diving deeper into the requirements. In terms of progress, we are now at the 1st chapter of 2. This first chapter is about the essentials: what's the history of these standards, what's the terminology, the assessment process, and other topics. Then, we'll dive deep into the 12 Requirements. Examining every single one of them, as well as what they demand.

What are our goals for this chapter? Well, the major one is to provide a brief introduction to the PCI-DSS. What are these standards, and how did they come to be? This includes specific topics such as: First, covering a brief history of the different versions of the PCI-DSS, as well as the reason for their creation. Then, clarifying the key terms of the framework, such as what is the CDE, or Card Data Environment, and what is CHD, or Cardholder Data, including SAD, which is Sensitive Authentication Data, among other acronyms. Also, clarifying how a payment is performed.

From start to finish. What are the three major steps, and what are the different parties involved, including the issuing bank of the cardholder, and the acquiring bank of the merchant. This is not essential to understanding the PCI-DSS, but it's good payment industry knowledge, in general. Or, for example, what's the assessment process for a merchant, or organization, in terms of complying with PCI-DSS, which usually occurs either with a Report on Compliance - an ROC -

or a Self-Assessment Questionnaire - an SAQ - as well as an overview of the different types of SAQs, which are 8 in total. In order to cover what the PCI-DSS are, we are going to touch on 4 major topics. The first is clarifying the terminology. What's the CDE, or Card Data Environment, what's CHD, or Cardholder Data, and more.

Then, we'll cover the history of the PCI-DSS. How they came to be, in 2004, why, as well as some of the major revisions since then. Then, we'll cover the merchant assessment process. What are the options for an organization that wishes to assess themselves, and what each option consists of. And, finally, we'll cover the anatomy of the payment flow. We'll cover what's the flow of a payment transaction, from start to finish, from authorization to settlement, and its three major stages. So, as you see, in this chapter, we are going to cover the basics of the PCI-DSS, before diving into more advanced territory. What are the common terms? What is the assessment process? And more.

Terminology Clarifications

Let's clarify the terminology of the PCI-DSS. There are a lot of terms, in the PCI-DSS, such as, for example, data, such as the CHD or the SAD - or, for example, the CDE, or Card Data Environment - and we even have terminology related to the assessment process itself, with the SAQs and the ROCs. So, let's take a moment just to cover all of these. Before proceeding with clarifying the PCI-DSS framework, it's important to clarify certain abbreviations and terms that show up over and over again. And these can be related to data, to networks, systems, and other elements. First, I want to clarify two terms, which are the CDE and CHD. So, the CDE, or Card Data Environment, is nothing more than the set of networks and systems where Cardholder Data, or CHD, is stored or transmitted.

As opposed to the rest of your systems and networks, which are the non-CDE, or Non-Card Data Environment. Let's put it in very simple terms. You're a coffee shop, and you have two Wi-Fi networks. Only one of these is used for payments. So that one is in the Card Data Environment. The other one is used for guests, for example. That one is not in the Card Data Environment (CDE). But the moment that card data is stored or transmitted in this other Wi-Fi, it immediately becomes part of the Card Data Environment. And by that same token, your Point of Sale, the database where you store the card data, or any paper records where you store or transmit card data are all in the CDE.

Actually, one of the practices before starting a PCI-DSS assessment is something called "scoping". And scoping is precisely determining the scope of the Card Data Environment. So, if you have 500 machines, 36 Wi-Fi networks, which of these store or transmit card data and which don't. And taking it one step further, after scoping, organizations usually try to reduce the scope of the Card Data Environment, because, remember, only that card data environment needs to comply with the PCI-DSS. In the same example, if one Wi-Fi is used for card data, and the other one is used for guests, then, obviously, the one for guests does not need to comply with the PCI-DSS.

So, in short, the Card Data Environment (CDE) is any system or network where your card data stays - or even passes through. That's the simple definition! And then, we have the CHD, or Cardholder Data itself. As you're probably guessing, these are the data on credit cards - or debit cards. As we'll see in a minute, this is not all credit card data. Only the one usually on the front. So account numbers, expiration dates, and others. Usually, the sensitive data - so, the PIN, the CVV code, and others that would allow an authorization by themselves are in a special category, which we'll see in a minute. And, as you're probably guessing, this Cardholder Data must be secured both in storage and in transit.

The presence of Cardholder Data (CHD) in a system or network is precisely what makes it part of the Card Data Environment (CDE). In terms of Cardholder Data, we can even go deeper and clarify what is the type of cardholder data that can be stored. What I mean by this is the following: There are usually 2 categories of data in a credit or debit card. Usually, the data on the front, and the data on the back. The data on the front can usually be stored and transmitted. It's the CHD. While the data on the back can only be transmitted - but never stored. That's the SAD, or Sensitive Authentication Data. So, first we have CHD, and CHD are usually the data on the front of the card.

So it includes, for example, the full card number, which has an acronym by itself - which is the PAN, or Personal Account Number - it's the full number on the card. Usually, you may see it masked when in transit. For example, the first 6 digits can be shown, as well as the last 4. Everything in the middle is the unique part, related to your account. Besides the Personal Account Number (PAN), we usually have the expiration date, and any other data that may be on the front. So, the cardholder name, the tier of the card, personal branding or identification, and more. And then, as mentioned, the SAD or Sensitive Authentication Data is usually the data on the back of the card.

So these are the data that would allow a transaction to be performed by themselves, and that's why they cannot be stored at all under PCI-DSS. Think of it this way: if a hacker steals the full account number - the full card number - that's bad. But if they steal the full card number AND the CVV code... that would be devastating for a company! So the SAD cannot be stored at all. It usually includes, first: The 3-digit card security number, which, depending on the brand, may be called the CVV number, the CVV2 number, the CVC number, or others - then the magnetic track itself, or the PIN number of the card. So, again, the biggest distinction is that Cardholder Data (CHD) can be stored and transmitted. Sensitive Authentication Data (SAD) can be transmitted, but never stored.

Otherwise, it's an immediate failure of compliance with PCI-DSS. Then, the PCI-DSS set of standards, by themselves, include 6 major goals, and 12 requirements. Each of the goals of the framework is usually associated with one or more requirements. There's a one-to-many relationship, if you will. For example, as of version 3.2.1, one of the goals is to "Build and maintain a secure network", and it contains both Requirement #1, which is to "Install and maintain a firewall configuration", and Requirement #2, which is to "Not use vendor-supplied defaults". And we'll take a look at these requirements in detail later, but for now, just realize that you have a set of goals, which are more theoretical, about the principles, and then the requirements, which are the specific manifestations of those goals.

So, again, while the goals are more generic, as I just mentioned - they're about the principles - the requirements are more technical, and explicit. Usually, with specific rules and procedures to be implemented. So, in this example, the goal is to "Build and maintain a secure network". It's generic. But, for example, in Requirement #1, you will have specific procedures in terms of changes to firewall configurations, the specific documents that must be produced - including network topology and cardholder flow diagram - authorization rules that deny users the ability to change their firewall settings, and so on. So, goals are generic, while requirements are very explicit. In many cases, organizations even ignore the goals and they just follow the requirements themselves - as a checklist.

So, while this is not necessarily the best approach - because you need to understand the rationale behind the requirements - it definitely can be done. The requirements can be checked, like boxes. It's also important to understand some terms related to the PCI-DSS compliance process itself. That is, when any merchant, or organization in general, wants to comply with the PCI-DSS, they have to actually assess themselves. And, for this purpose, merchants usually have two mechanisms: An ROC, or Report on Compliance, and an SAQ, or Self-Assessment Questionnaire. The ROC - or Report on Compliance - involves an assessor actually visiting the company, and doing a lengthy examination. The SAQ, or Self-Assessment Questionnaire exists as 8 types in total.

And the organization fills the questionnaire - so, one of those 8 types - that corresponds to how they deal with card data. For example, a company that completely outsources card data has to reply to completely different questions than a company that actually stores card data, or another one that just uses a local POS, and doesn't even connect to the Internet. And we'll take a look at this in more detail later - but what defines whether a merchant is forced to perform an ROC

- or whether they can actually just fill an SAQ - is whether they are a Level 1 merchant or not. That is, there are 4 levels of merchants, based on the volume of yearly transactions. Not the value, the VOLUME of transactions. And any merchant that processes more than 6 million transactions per year is immediately a Level 1 merchant, and they must take an ROC.

All other levels of merchants can just fill an SAQ. Furthermore, ROCs are usually performed by professionals called QSAs, or Qualified Security Assessors. These are independent and certified security auditors that go into an organization, examine their practices, and security controls, and they produce a report, detailing what they comply with, and what they don't. And, out of curiosity, the QSAs themselves don't just perform full ROCs. They can be useful even for SAQs. For example, they can provide some sort of consulting service to an organization helping them select the right type of SAQ that they must fill.

Because, as we'll cover letter, taking the wrong SAQ for your organization can be very costly, because you can answer a lot more questions than you need to, and you can also fail compliance, because the questionnaire that you pick may neglect some area which was actually needed. But, to summarize, it's either an ROC or an SAQ. If the merchant is a Level 1 merchant - that is, 6 million transactions or more per year - it must take an ROC, with a physical visit from an assessor. Otherwise, it can just take an SAQ, that is filled and delivered to their bank - or their card company, if they're a payment processor. And they have to pick the right type of SAQ out of the 8 types. And finally, there are some terms that are important to be aware of in terms of payments in general.

Any payment professional will be aware of these, but some may not be familiar with the industry, so it's important to clarify these. So, in any transaction, or payment, between a consumer and a merchant, there are usually two banks involved. One of them is the issuing bank that issued the card of the cardholder - or consumer - and the other is the acquiring bank, which is the bank where the merchant has an account. For example, you may hear about these in terms of fraud or dispute cases. If there's fraud on the credit card, then the issuer bank of that card performs an investigation, because the card was issued by them. And in a chargeback process, it's believed that the cardholder deserves their money back.

So the issuing bank performs what's called a "chargeback", which is a request of the acquiring bank to give the money back. So, these are two important terms. PCI-DSS is a type of compliance that is demanded of merchants by their acquiring banks. So, if I have an accounting firm, for example, and I have an account at HSBC, then they will be the ones requiring that I be PCI-DSS certified. And if it's a Self-Assessment Questionnaire, or SAQ, then I fill it and I deliver it to the bank. It's important to note that PCI-DSS is not legal regulation. It's industry regulation. So if a merchant doesn't comply with it, the government is not going to go after them.

They don't break the law. But the bank, themselves, may impose fees on them, or fines, or even fire them as a customer. Or the card company can do so as well. And, finally, the handling of Cardholder Data (CHD) by the merchant can be performed in a CP, or Card Present environment - which is, for example, what happens if you're paying through a terminal in a shop, for example, in a Starbucks coffee shop, usually with a PIN number for authentication - or in a Card Non-Present environment, or CNP. And this is, for example, buying online on Amazon. And it usually uses the CVV number for authorization. What are some examples of these terms? The first is choosing the right SAQ.

There are 8 different types of SAQ, as we mentioned, and these depend on how the company handles Cardholder Data. Whether they store it or not, how they transmit it, whether the card is present, not present, and so on. Then, as mentioned, PCI-DSS is industrial compliance, not legal. In this case, it's not demanded by the law, but demanded by the merchant's acquiring bank. Or, if you are a service provider, instead of a merchant, it's usually the card company itself, instead of a bank. And, again, failing it is not breaking the law. But it can still have grave penalties, including fines, sanctions, payment limitations, or in a worst-case scenario, actually being fired by your bank or card company.

And finally, the Card Data Environment being reduced is a practice. As we mentioned, the CDE, or Card Data Environment, is what defines what needs to be PCI-DSS certified. So, a frequent practice is for companies to reduce the scope of the CDE as much as possible, because the less systems or networks that handle card data, the smaller the scope of compliance. If you have 26 Wi-Fi networks, having your card data go through one of them, versus all 26, is brutal! It's the difference in having to comply with firewall configurations, logging configurations, Intrusion Detection Systems (IDS), File Integrity Monitoring (FIM), and many other requirements (which we'll check) in one network versus 26. So, organizations are always looking to reduce the CDE.

What are our key takeaways here? The first is the CDE and the non-CDE. The set of systems and networks that deal with Cardholder Data (CHD), that is, that store it or transmit it, are the Card Data Environment, or CDE. All other systems and networks are non-CDE. Then, Cardholder Data can be split into CHD or SAD. Cardholder Data is usually the information on the front of the card. It can be stored and transmitted. SAD, or Sensitive Authentication Data, is usually the data on the back. CVV numbers, the magnetic track, PIN numbers, and it absolutely cannot be stored. Just transmitted. The PCI-DSS, as a set of standards, have 6 goals and 12 requirements.

Each goal has one or more requirements associated. While the goals are more general, and they represent principles, the requirements are very declarative and technical by nature. They're things like saying, "You need unique IDs for users", "You need change management for all firewall rule changes", "You need risk assessment once a year with an output", and so on. Then, PCI-DSS compliance can be achieved through a Report on Compliance, or a Self-Assessment Questionnaire. It all depends on whether you are a Level 1 merchant or not. If you have more than 6 million transactions per year, you are Level 1, and you require a Report on Compliance, with a physical visit from a QSA.

If you aren't, then you can perform a Self-Assessment Questionnaire, which is usually one of 8 types. And, finally, there are some useful terms in terms of the payment industry itself. In any transaction between a cardholder and a merchant, the bank of the merchant is known as the "acquiring bank", and the bank of the cardholder is known as the "issuing bank". And the card company is usually the intermediary between both. So, as you see, it's important to master all of these terms. You don't need to memorize them right away, but they are going to show up over and over. And it's important to understand, within each context, what they actually mean. What is CHD or SAD, in terms of data? What is the CDE, in terms of the environment Versus the non-CDE? And more.

PCI-DSS History

Let's talk about the history of the PCI-DSS. You can skip this chapter, if you want, but it is important to get the historical context of this type of regulation. We are going to focus on the last working version, which is version 3.2.1. Although version 4.0.0 has just come out, it has not been tested yet, and there's still going to be a lot of feedback. So 3.2.1 is the last "proven" one - which is very similar to 4.0.0. But, anyway, let's take a look at all of the different versions so far, and just a brief history of what the PCI-DSS are, how they came to be, and what is their goal. PCI-DSS are also known as the Payment Card Industry Data Security Standards. Out of curiosity, they're a plural name, that's why you don't hear me saying "PCI-DSS is", but you hear me saying, "The PCI-DSS are".

The standards! They are a set of directives for how credit - or debit - card data should be stored and transmitted securely by organizations. And these organizations can be banks, service providers, merchants, or any other company that processes card data. They were created - and they're maintained - by the PCI SSC, or the Payment Card Industry Security Standards Council. They are the ones that push out new versions and gather feedback. As of today, in November 2021, PCI-DSS are in version 3.2.1, with version 4.0 expected to be released in the first quarter of 2022. Historically, the first version was released in 2004.

Before these unified standards, every single card company, such as VISA, MasterCard, and so on had their own security standards - and, as you're probably guessing, this made it very difficult for merchants wanting to accept payments from multiple companies. It's precisely why the PCI-DSS were created. It was a unified effort to create a single set of security standards. So, as mentioned, at the time of its creation, in 2004, payment fraud was rising considerably. And, to be honest, in 2021, it hasn't really slowed down, unfortunately. And this was the big catalyst for the representatives of all these major card companies to come together in order to define one single set of standards on how to transmit and store card data. The goal was to simplify compliance, so that merchants could fight fraud more easily. And, since 2004, these standards continue to evolve in every release.

And they have gone through some pretty big iterations! For, example, version 1.1 introduced the firewall requirement - which is now Requirement #1, as of version 3.2.1 - which is about controlling traffic, denying unidentified traffic, requiring change management for firewall rules, and so on. Version 1.2 established standards for antivirus software, requiring that the software exists, be regularly updated, scan regularly, and so on, to prevent malware. And every version brings with it new changes. So the standards evolve with the safety requirements of the industry, as over time, there are new types of attacks, new technology, and so on. Any new release of the PCI-DSS is a very organic process. It's very agile by nature, and it has its own lifecycle.

So, usually the transition lasts for 3 years - at least, in the current version 3.2.1. So, what happens is that, in the 1st year, the standards are published. So it's the first revision of that version. And they're effective for companies. And implementation of these begins. In the 2nd year, the standards council receives the initial feedback from the early adopters, and they use that feedback in order to revise this version, which is then reviewed. The 2nd year is also when the previous standards start to be retired. So they exist in parallel, but by the 2nd year, they start to be phased out. And, finally, the 3rd year is mostly about maintenance.

So, the standards are revised - again, according to feedback - and they reach the final version, which is published, and all organizations, by the

3rd year, adopt the new version, and retire the previous one. What are some examples? The first is fraud. A present danger. The reason why the PCI-DSS were created in the first place is still very much a threat. And that is payment fraud. Not only has payment fraud not slowed down with new technology, and the move to digital - for example, since, COVID-19 - it has only accelerated, and continues on the rise. Then, unfortunately, the PCI-DSS is adopted by a low percentage of organizations. As of 2020, only 27.9% of global organizations had adopted the PCI-DSS.

That's less of a third! And this means that there's still a large number of merchants that are vulnerable to fraud. More than 2/3rds! And, finally, out of curiosity, one radical revision was version 3.0. And it brought along penetration testing. So, before version 3.0, merchants didn't really need to care about hacking. They could just do small vulnerability scans. But, after version 3.0, specific and major rules around vulnerability scanning, penetration testing, intrusion detection systems, and others were implemented. What are our key takeaways here? The first is that the PCI Security Standards Council was formed by representatives of the different card companies. They came together looking to standardize the directives for card data transfer and card data storage - which are the DSS, or Data Security Standards.

Then, the PCI-DSS continually evolves in each iteration. Both based on the feedback received, from earlier versions, by the early implementers, but also new trends in technology and attacks. And, finally, every version of the PCI-DSS, as of 3.2.1, has a 3-year lifecycle. In the 1st year, the standards are implemented, and feedback is collected. In year 2, that feedback is reviewed and the old standards start to be retired. In year 3, the final revision of this version comes, and the old standards are completely retired. So, as we see, the PCI-DSS have been through some major revisions since they were originally created, to standardize how credit cards are protected across different brands. And don't forget that each iteration of the PCI-DSS is based on real-world market feedback. And each version usually has a lifecycle of 3 years.

Merchant Assessment

Let's talk about merchant assessment, or organizational assessment. When any organization wants to assess itself, in terms of complying with the PCI-DSS, they can fill an SAQ - or Self-Assessment Questionnaire - or have an ROC - or Report on Compliance. But, there are criteria to define whether we take one or the other, and even within the SAQs, there are 8 different types. So, let's take a look at how this works. So, in terms of assessing yourself, as an organization, for the PCI-DSS, there are 2 possibilities for what may be required. As we just mentioned. The first alternative is an SAQ, or Self-Assessment Questionnaire, while the second is an ROC, or Report on Compliance. The major difference between these two is that the SAQs are performed by the organization itself.

That is, you fill a questionnaire, and then you deliver it to your bank - so, they are simpler and they are faster, at the end of the day - while the ROCs have to be performed by a Qualified Security Assessor, or QSA - that is, an assessor, who is a specialist in the PCI-DSS, goes into your organization and takes a look at what you're doing well - and, more often, at what you're not! So, as you're probably thinking, in every case, where you can choose an SAQ, it's a better alternative, because it's faster, it costs less, and it demands just less work, at the end of the day.

And here's the key: How do you define whether to do one or the other? So, the major criterion that defines whether an organization needs an ROC, or on the other hand, whether an SAQ is actually acceptable, is very simple: If they are a Level 1 merchant - that is, if they have more than 6 million transactions per year - they need an ROC. Period. All other types of merchants - which are Levels 2, 3 and 4, as we'll see in a minute - can take an SAQ. Before we proceed, let's just cover the four levels of merchants very quickly, from big to small. So, Level 1 merchants process more than 6 million transactions per year. And this is not dependent on the value of the transaction - it can be $1 or $1M - they just have to be more than 6 million transactions themselves.

Then come Level 2 merchants, which process between 1 million and 6 million transactions per year. Then, the 3rd category are Level 3 merchants, which process between 20,000 and 1 million transactions per year. And, finally, we have Level 4 merchants. And these process less than 20,000 transactions per year. And, as mentioned, any merchant from Level 2 to 4 - so, these 3 categories - can perform a Self-Assessment Questionnaire - which is submitted to their acquiring bank, if they are merchants, or submitted to the card company directly, if they're a payment processor. But the Level 1 merchants must take a Report on Compliance in a mandatory manner. There's no way out. And it must be performed by a QSA.

In other words, if you process more than 6 million transactions per year, you must take a Report on Compliance. And if you process any level below that, you can just fill a Self-Assessment Questionnaire. Now, here is the thing: even for these merchants from level 2-4 taking the SAQ, itself, is not that simple. And the reason for this is that there are 8 types available. And these depend on the type of organization, and how they handle cardholder data (CHD). There's a few groups for merchants that handle Card Non-Present (CNP) transactions versus Card Present (CP) transactions. And two types which are global.

So, first, for Card Not-Present transactions, the first is the SAQ-A, which is for fully outsourced payments. You have a website that redirects to PayPal, for example, and the SAQ-A-EP, which is for partially outsourced merchants. This is, for example, where you do have a third party for payments, but you communicate the card data through an HTTP POST request, for example. So it does pass by your website. That's the difference between these two. We'll take a look at this in more detail later on, but the rule of thumb is that websites are either SAQ-A, SAQ-A-EP, or SAQ-D. You immediately fall into SAQ-D if you store card data. Otherwise, you fit into one of these previous ones. But I'm getting ahead of myself! Next comes the SAQ-C.

So, these are payment apps connected to the Internet. They're not websites per se, but they're specific applications that are simply connected to the Internet, for only one purpose - to communicate transactions. For example, the SAQ-C-VT, in specific, is for isolated virtual payments, by mail or telephone. Think of someone in a call center, that's taking in credit card data, over the phone, and posting that on a website, through a very specific secure connection. Then, for Card Present transactions, we have, first, the SAQ-B, which is for "old machines". Really! It's for imprint machines that take a carbon copy of your card - very old ones - or terminals that are connected by dial connections. For example, in small newspaper shops.

The SEQ-B-IP is for PTS-approved terminals that connect through an IP connection - therefore the "IP". These are approved by PTS standards, and they're payment terminals that connect via IP, via an internet connection. Then, we have the SAQ-P2PE. This is for hardware terminals that are managed by P2PE systems (or peer-to-peer encryption systems). These terminals are special. They use strong encryption, and they have their own SAQ. They're kind of the sophisticated version of these two. And then we have the catch-all category, the SAQ-D. This is the category for merchants - or providers - that don't fit any other category.

If you can avoid being categorized as SAQ-D, you are going to want that! Because - we'll see this in a minute - but, while every other one of these has between 40 and 80 questions, the SAQ-D has around 300! That's right. And, out of curiosity, if you store card data you immediately jump to this category. Every other category is for devices or systems that only transmit card data, and don't store it. So, the SAQ-D can be for service providers - which are, for example, providers of machines, payment terminals, and so on, and the SAQ-D for merchants, which are all merchants that don't fit into any of the previous categories.

So, it's important to note that different SAQ types demand compliance with different requirements. And they also have a different total number of questions. For example, the SAQ for the P2P encryption machines only fits requirements 3, 9, and 12, which are, respectively, to store data securely, to restrict physical access, and to have an information security policy. They're payment machines, so other requirements, including firewalls and antivirus, just don't apply to them. So, although we will cover the 12 requirements, in this Book, depending on your SAQ, you may not need to obey all of them.

So, the SAQ-A, for outsourced payments, has to comply with requirements 2, 8, 9, and 12 - that is, related to vendor defaults, access control, user identification, physical access control, and an information security policy. And it only has 22 questions. If you use a third party for all payments, there's not a lot that you have to answer! The SAQ-A-EP is different. It has to comply with all 12 requirements. And it has 193 questions. So, the difference between fully integrating the third party for payments, or partially integrating it is quite big! Then, the SAQ-B, which is for imprint machines, and dial-out terminals, has requirements 3, 4, 7, 9, and 12, which have to do with securing stored data, securing transmitted data, logical access control, physical access control, and having an information security policy.

And it's just 41 questions. If it's a terminal that connects by IP, then you have all requirements except 5 and 10, and the questions are 84. The SAQ-C, which is for payment apps connected to the internet, naturally, has all requirements, and 162 questions. And the

SAQ-C-VT, which is for phone or mail orders that use a web portal, has less questions - 81, in specific - because it's a specific type - and one less requirement. The SAQ-D, as we mentioned, is the worst case scenario. If you get included in this category, you comply with all 12 requirements, and you answer 332 questions - whether as a merchant or payment provider. And, finally, the SAQ for peer-to-peer encryption hardware (P2PE-HW) machines only complies with requirements 3, 9, and 12 - which is storing encrypted data, physical protection of the data, and having an information security policy.

And it only contains 33 questions - and, by the way, you can come back to this chapter after we've covered the requirements - and there are many other variations of this table online, but if anything, what I want you to take away is that how you transmit and store data immediately affects the type of questionnaire that you can fill. It has implications in terms of your compliance - and the actual work in filling these questionnaires! We can also go a little bit deeper into the categories, before finishing the chapter. So Category A, as mentioned, is fully outsourced e-commerce merchants. So, your website doesn't touch cards. All the processing of payments is done either through an iFrame or a redirect to a third party. And this is the most straightforward type of SAQ. Merchants aim to be in this category.

Then SAQ-A-EP, as mentioned, is partially outsourced web portals. So, the card data is not stored, but it is transmitted. And just that fact imposes a lot of compliance on you! You may be using, for example, an HTTP POST form to redirect to the third party. In this scenario, no card data even passes through your system. In this scenario, it may pass only in one type of request, but that's enough to change the category! SAQ-B, as mentioned, is for the "old machines". So, these are dial-out merchants, for example, which are chip or PIN devices connected via phone, or old imprint machines, which take a carbon copy of the credit card. None of these store information, and in these cases, the physical security of the machines - or paper copies - is the focus.

So, the PCI-DSS focuses both on digital security and physical security. And this is one category where digital security is almost irrelevant. There's no databases, no digital transmission, however, the physical copies have to be secured as well. Then, SAQ-B-IP is exactly the same as for this one, but it's for standalone payment terminals or chip devices that use an IP connection. So, there's an additional focus on everything else related to internet communication. So, firewalls, encrypted storage, encrypted transmission... The only two that are not included are antivirus and penetration testing, and I'm guessing that's because the machines don't need them.

If they did, those requirements would be here as well! Then, C-VT, as a subcategory of SAQ-C, is for web-based virtual terminals. These are terminals that you see in shops or call centers, where there is direct entry of payment information. The person takes the credit card details and inputs them in a console. But it's not a browser. It's one specific connection through one specific device. The card data is also not stored. By the way, as I mentioned, if any merchant stores data, they immediately get slotted into D. So, for C-VT, this device, naturally, must be isolated in the network, because, otherwise, the rest of the network where the device is in becomes in scope of the PCI-DSS, which is something that you don't want! You want the Card Data Environment (CDE) to be only this network, with only this connection.

Then, Category C are payment app systems that are connected to the internet. So, the payment processing is in the device itself - it's not an internet app - but the device connects to the internet. There's also no storage. Then, SAQ-D, as mentioned, is the kitchen sink. All other merchants and all payment provider brands land here. It's important to note, as mentioned, that any merchant that stores data immediately lands in this category. For example, e-commerce merchants are usually A, A-EP or D. If they fully outsource their payment, they're A. If they partially outsource it they're A-EP. If they store card data. They are D. And, as mentioned, category P2PE-HW is for merchants that have hardware payment terminals, but specific ones - PCI-validated peer-to-peer encryption chip or PIN devices.

And, again, no card data storage. Otherwise, they would be category D. It's important to note, in closing, that an organization may meet multiple criteria for multiple SAQs. For example, if they have multiple payment systems, which are different. And, in that case, they must take all of the corresponding SAQs, in that case. This is completely normal, and it occurs. So if you have both a website that is partially outsourced, and a hardware peer-to-peer encryption machine, you must fill both SAQ-A-EP and SEQ-P2PE. It's also important to note that selecting the wrong SAQ for an organization may result in failing PCI-DSS compliance.

This is because usually, when you fill the wrong questionnaire, you may ignore requirements that actually apply to you. So, you may fill an SAQ that doesn't have Requirement #1, about firewalls, but it actually applies to you. So, you fail because you don't fill it. Out of curiosity, if you choose an SAQ that is more inclusive. you don't fail, because you're complying with everything you need and more! But, usually, when people fail, it's because they choose an SAQ that is simpler, not more complex! And the consequences of failing PCI-DSS can range from something called compensating controls (which is when the assessor recommends extra measures for you to be able to comply - for example, if your firewall is fine, but you don't use change management for the rules, they may suggest that, as a compensating control) to other consequences such as fines, or even removal of payment brand association.

So, in severe cases, for example, VISA may turn to a merchant, and say, "You can't take VISA cards for payment anymore". But even if there's nothing else, you may just waste time filling the wrong SAQ. Because, remember, the number of questions can range from 30 to around 300. If instead of taking an SAQ with 40 questions, you take SAQ-D, with 330, you almost answer 10 times as many questions, for no purpose. So, what are some examples here? The first is that validation is required, in some cases. That is, usually, the bank requests their merchant client to have the SAQ filled, and they just accept it when it's delivered. But if this specific bank has suspicions of this specific merchant, or if they just want to be extra sure, they can request the SAQ to be validated by a QSA.

Then, as we mentioned, online merchants are usually A, A-EP, or D. And this is depending on their activities. That is, they are either fully outsourced - which is SAQ A - they're partially outsourced - which is A-EP - or, if they store data, they are SAQ-D. And, finally, Level 1 merchants are based on the transaction volume, and not value. For example, Level 1 means more than 6 million in transactions, but it doesn't matter if any particular transaction is of 1 million or 1 dollar, because what matters here is security. If a credit card is compromised, then the whole balance of that card is compromised. So it doesn't matter if a purchase is $1, or $1 million - that account is still compromised, if the credit card number is compromised itself.

That's why only the transaction volume matters - which is the number of credit cards which are exposed. So, what are our key takeaways this time? The first is that, in order to be assessed, merchants will fit one of four levels. And only Level 1 merchants - which is, more than 6 million in transactions, per year - must take an ROC - a Report on Compliance. All other merchants can just get away with filling an SAQ and delivering it to their bank. Then, remember: There are 8 different SAQs.

Depending on their activities, merchants must take 1 of 8 different SAQ types. A and A-EP - which are website with outsourced payments - B or B-IP - which are for dial-out or IP terminals - C or C-VT - which are isolated virtual terminals - D - which is everything else - or P2PE, for Peer-to-Peer Encrypted Machines. And, naturally, the most extensive and miscellaneous one, if you will, is SAQ-D. And, finally, there are different requirements depending on the SAQ. Although we have 12 requirements in total, for PCI-DSS compliance - as of version 3.2.1, depending on the SAQ that they fill, the merchants may not have to comply with all 12 requirements. This has to do with their types of systems and networks, such as, for example, payment terminals not needing antivirus (which is Requirement #5).

So, as we see, when an organization is assessing itself, it must fill an SAQ or take an ROC. And this is only defined by whether they are a Level 1 merchant or not. That is, over 6 million transactions per year, or not. And remember, even if they take an SAQ, it can be of 8 different types, and the type of SAQ actually defines the number of requirements that you have to comply with, with the "worst" type being the SAQ-D, with all requirements!

Anatomy of a Payment Flow

Let's cover the anatomy of a payment flow. If you are a payment professional, you may already know about this. But some information security professionals, who may be undertaking the PCI-DSS, may not know about this. So, what we're going to cover are the 3 major stages of any payment. That is, the authentication, the authorisation, and the clearing and settlement. And how the different entities, such as the issuing bank and acquiring bank interact with each other. Let's take a look. Let's cover the anatomy of a payment flow. That is, any payment, from a consumer, to a merchant, relative to a transaction, or a purchase in specific, of a product or service, has always 3 major stages.

And this may be obvious to anybody who is a payment professional already, but some people may not be aware of it in detail - and you can skip it if you want. But these 3 stages are the authentication, the authorisation, and the clearing and settlement. It's also important to clarify the major parties themselves, involved in the payment. These are, first of all, the consumer. Who is also known as the cardholder, because they usually pay for a purchase with a card (if they're not paying with card, then it's usually a type of payment fraud that doesn't matter to us, or that works in a similar manner to a purchase with a card). And then, representing them, we usually have what is called the issuing bank. It's the bank of the consumer, and it's called the issuing bank because they've issued the consumer's card.

And, on the other hand, we have the merchant, on the other side of the transaction. And we have what is called the "acquiring bank", or the merchant bank. That is, the bank of this merchant, where they are a client. And, finally, we usually have the card company itself, of the specific card which is used, who acts as an intermediary to both parties. And this may be VISA, MasterCard, and etc. So, usually, you have a transfer of capital from the issuing bank to the acquiring bank, through the card company, representing that purchase, made by the cardholder from the merchant. So, the general process, in diagram form, is the following: First, we have the authentication.

This is when the merchant sends the details of the transaction to the acquirer bank, which then sends them to the card company. For example, you buy a coffee at Starbucks, and you put your VISA card in the POS, and this is when the merchant sends the details of the transaction, to be able to charge you $7, for example. Then, the second step is authorisation. This is when VISA actually sends the request to charge those $7, and it goes from VISA to your issuing bank, which authorizes it - or not! And, if they authorize it, you get a receipt, and there is a hold on your account, for those $7, which may be taken away sooner or later. And, when they're taken away, then the third step is precisely this, which is called the clearing and settlement.

These are two distinct back office operations. So, usually, at the end of the day, or within 24 hours, at a specific period, the merchant - for example, the Starbucks in our example - sends all transactions to their acquirer bank, which sends them to the card company - which, in turn, sends them to the issuer bank of every single customer. For example, the payment for your coffee, and for all others from VISA customers go to VISA. Starbucks sends those transactions to VISA. Then, VISA sends these transactions to the individual issuing bank of every customer who made a purchase, including your bank, for that purchase with your card.

And then, that bank makes the transfer, through VISA, back to Starbucks's bank. And VISA usually takes a cut in this process. So, this is the general flow of a payment. So, let's elaborate a little bit more on these steps. So, the first step, authentication, is all about the merchant communicating the transaction to the card company. They're authenticating themselves as someone who can charge you this money, if you will. So, again, in our example, when you buy something, with a VISA card, and you see on the terminal, "$19.99, enter PIN" - or whatever amount - then, the merchant is authenticating themselves and then, they will request authorisation to charge that money - which is the step that comes after. And then, their bank will communicate this to VISA.

So, the second step is authorisation. And it's all about the bank of the cardholder accepting the charge. So, the first step was about the merchant communicating with VISA. And in this step, it's about VISA communicating with your bank, and getting the charge authorized. Therefore the name. So, when you see on the POS, "Processing", and you later see "Accepted" - hopefully! - after entering the PIN, what's happening is that VISA got the request from the merchant to charge you this amount, and now they're translating that request to your bank, to authorize them to take away the money, and the bank may authorize it - if there's enough balance, or the account is OK, otherwise - but, if it's not authorized, then the whole process just stops here, and you see a "Declined" message.

Or some other sort of error message. Otherwise, if the transaction is authorized, you see "Accepted" on the machine, then a hold is placed on your account for those $19.99, and you immediately get a paper receipt on the POS. The third step is clearing and settlement. These are two common transaction back office operations, and they usually occur within 24 or 48 hours. The reason why they're not immediate is due to a process called "netting", but that's an entirely different topic of financial transaction back office operations. For payment purchases, you just need to know that your money is captive, and it will be taken between 24 to 48 hours. So what are clearing and settlement, in specific? By definition, clearing means that, at some point, the issuing bank will verify that you have the capital, that you are the account owner, and other simple checks.

So, that authorization that you granted on the machine was a temporary one. The bank doesn't know that this transaction was really authorized by you. So, later on, they will make some basic checks on your account, and then do what's called "clearing" the transaction. As the name says, it's "clear" to proceed. Then, we have a settlement. Settlement comes after this, and it's the final, legal, settlement of the ledgers. What I mean is that, legally, your bank account now has -$19.99 - it's on the electronic ledger - while the merchant's ledger has +$19.99. Minus whatever commission the card company takes. But, anyways, this is the final movement in the banks' ledgers. It's the legal change of possession of that capital.

So, what happens is that, at the end of the day, usually, the merchant will send all transactions - including your specific one of $19.99 - to the acquiring bank. In our example, Starbucks takes all transactions and sends them to their bank. And their acquiring bank, in turn, sends all of those transactions to their card companies. For example, all VISA transactions to VISA. All MasterCard transactions to MasterCard. And so on. And what happens is that the card company, such as VISA, charges every single one of the issuing banks. So they call your bank and they say, "We are going to charge $19.99". They call another bank, or another customer, and say, "We are going to charge (whatever it is)".

So they charge all the issuing banks for the card purchases - or at least, all authorized ones! - and then they deposit that value to the respective acquirer bank - for example, Starbucks's bank. And they usually take a fee from this movement. What are some examples of the payment flow? The first are chargebacks. Chargebacks occur when a customer believes that they have been tricked or defrauded. So, in this case, their issuing bank performs what is called a "chargeback", which formally is the name given to the formal request, by an issuing bank, that the acquirer bank return their money. So, again, in our example, you go to Starbucks, but you don't buy anything, and you still get charged $7.

Maybe they say it's free due to a coupon, but you have to put your card anyway, and you get charged. So, you call your bank, then the bank starts a "chargeback" process, where they will contact Starbucks's bank, and say, "Hey, give us this money back". Then, netting is one of the major reasons for the timeframe of clearing. And the process of netting is very simple. Throughout this period, of 1 or 2 days, there are multiple transactions, right? Some +, some -. So these are usually grouped, and only the net is transacted. For example, imagine you have Santander and HSBC. In that 24-hour period, maybe there's a $100 million transfer from Santander to HSBC from some purchases, but maybe there is another one from HSBC to Santander of $200 million.

You can perform that $100 million transaction one way, and the other $200 million one the other way... or you can just meet them, which results in a total of $100 million from HSBC to Santander. And you only perform that transaction. So this lowers the number of transactions, and the costs. Pretty much you're saying, "Instead of doing all these movements, from one bank to the other, let's just calculate the net, and let's just transfer that!". In terms of payments, this isn't a big cost saver, but, for example, in the capital markets, it's gigantic. You will have hundreds of thousands of transactions within one day, where one bank has to transfer $1 million, get $2 million, transfer another million, get another 10, and it's much simpler to just wait until the period is over, and transfer the net result.

It's that simple! But, again, this only works if there's a 24- to 48-hour period. Because, if this would be immediate, you would not net them. They would be cleared as they happen. So you have to actually wait, in order for this to be an advantage.This is just out of curiosity, and it's a completely different topic, but it's the reason why clearing takes so long. And, finally, transactions may be not authorized. In the second stage of authorization, if the customer doesn't have enough balance - or there's another problem, for example, with a merchant - authorization can be rejected. And, in that case, the whole process simply stops there. So, what are our key takeaways here? The first is that there are 3 major stages in the payment process.

The first is authentication, when the merchant authenticates themselves and asks the card company, such as VISA, permission to charge the amount. Then, the second is authorisation, which is when the card company, such as VISA, asks the customer's bank - the issuing bank - to charge their card. And then, clearing and settlement, which is when the final value is credited, to the acquiring bank, from the issuing bank, and the ledgers are updated. Then, there are 3 major entities in this process. One is the issuing bank, of the cardholder, who issued the card, then the acquiring bank, or merchant bank, representing the merchant, and the card company - such as VISA or MasterCard - who intermediates the transaction.

And, then, remember: Clearing and settlement. These are two transaction back office operations, which are not the same, but are related. Clearing a transaction means performing the final checks to allow the funds to be transferred - as the name says, the transaction is "clear" to proceed - while settling means adjusting the ledgers on both sides. The legal ownership of the money, in the records, is now changed. So, as we see, we have 3 major stages, and many parties involved. The authentication stage, between the merchant and the card company, the authorisation stage, between the card company and the cardholder, and the clearing and settlement, where the money actually flows from the cardholder to the merchant.

Essentials Chapter

With this, we reach the end of the Essentials chapter, where we tried to cover the basic terminology - and basic definitions - of the PCI-DSS, before going deeper. Let's take a look at the topics that we've covered in this chapter. We are now at the end of the PCI-DSS Essentials chapter, where we covered the basics of these standards. In order to cover this framework, we touched on four major topics. The first were terminology clarifications. The common terms in the PCI-DSS. What is the CDE, or Card Data Environment, what is CHD, or Cardholder Data, what is SAD, or Sensitive Authentication Data, and, in terms of assessment, what is an ROC, or Report on Compliance, and an SAQ, or a Self-Assessment Questionnaire, as well as the QSA, or Qualified Security Assessor who can help you.

Then, we covered the history of the PCI-DSS. Founded in 2004, motivated by increases in payment fraud, and currently with a 3-year release lifecycle. Then, merchant assessment. The levels of merchants, and whether you need to take a Report on Compliance or just fill an SAQ, and which specific type of SAQ. Hopefully, not the SAQ-D! And finally, we analyzed payment flows. How a payment transaction occurs, from authorisation to authentication, and then clearing and settlement. Some questions that you can ask yourself to consolidate the knowledge in this chapter, as of version 3.2.1.of the PCI-DSS, include: First, how many different types of SAQs exist? And I guess I answered this one in the previous chapter, but answer it from memory! Also, what is the lengthiest SAQ that merchants look to avoid? What is the difference between Cardholder Data (CHD).

and Sensitive Authentication Data (SAD), in terms of storage and transmission? What is forbidden for which of these two types? What defines a Level 1 Merchant? And what consequences does that have for the assessment process? How many years does the release cycle of a new PCI-DSS version have? Again, I think I answered it in the previous chapter, but use your memory! And what happens, in general, in each of these years? Finally, out of the issuing bank and acquiring bank, which of the two represents a cardholder in the payment process? And also, who is the intermediary between these two banks? With this, we close the Essentials chapter, where we covered the basics of the PCI-DSS.

Welcome

Welcome to the 12 Requirements chapter. As of version 3.2.1, the PCI-DSS has 12 requirements. And, in this chapter, we are going to cover every single one of them, in detail. Let's take a look at the different topics for this chapter. We are now at the 12 Requirements chapter, where we are going to cover each requirement of the PCI-DSS, in detail. In terms of progress, very simple. We are in the 2nd chapter of 2. In the first chapter, we covered the essentials of the PCI-DSS. The history, the terminology, the assessment process, and so on. Now, we are at the 12 Requirements chapter. We will cover what each requirement means, and what it demands of the organization. Our major goal in this chapter is clarification. Clarifying all the 12 requirements of the PCI-DSS.

And this includes, among other elements: Clarifying Requirements #1 and #2, about securing networks with a firewall (Requirement 1) and removing defaults from devices - default passwords, accounts, and etc (Requirement 2). Then, Requirements #3 and #4, which are about protecting both stored data and transmitted data. #3 is about stored data, and #4 is about transmitted data. Then, Requirements #5 and #6, about securing machines. Requirement 5 is about securing machines with an antivirus software, to prevent malware, and Requirement 6 is about securing development itself. Identifying vulnerabilities in applications, developing securely, and patching vulnerabilities.

Then, Requirements #7 through #9 are about physical and digital security, as well as proper identification of user actions. Making sure that you can track an action back to an unique user. Then, Requirements #10 and #11 are about logging possible attacks - and logging everything, pretty much! - that's Requirement #10 - as well as protecting yourself from attacks, Requirement #11, regular testing.

And finally, clarifying Requirement #12, which is about having an Information Security policy. To properly cover the 12 Requirements, we will cover 14 chapters total. I know this sounds like a tall number, but it's essentially one chapter for the overview, then 12 requirements, then one recap chapter. So, first is an overview. Telling you what each requirement is about.

Then, we'll dive deep into the first requirement. Having a firewall. Protecting your Card Data Environment from dangerous traffic, having network documentation, proper change management for firewall rules, and more. Requirement #2 is about no defaults. Removing default passwords, default connection strings, default accounts, and more, because this information is public on the Internet. It's also about removing unneeded functionality that may represent a vulnerability. Then, Requirement #3 is about protecting stored data. Both on databases, but also on paper. It's about strong encryption, masking, tokenizing, hashing, and any possible measure to obscure the data. Requirement #4 is about securing transmitted data. It encrypts your communications, so that credit card data is secure across public channels.

Requirement #5 is very simple. No malware. Having antivirus software, keeping it updated, and keeping it running. Requirement #6 is about secure development and patches. Making sure that your developers take security requirements into account, as well as having a process for patching known vulnerabilities. Requirement #7 is about need-to-know access. Minimizing access to Cardholder Data (CHD) by your personnel. In short, the least people required have access to the data, and each person has the least access required to do their job. Then, Requirement #8 is the flip side of the previous one. It's about identifying access. Making sure that every action can be traced back to a specific user. Measures include forcing unique IDs, for every personnel member, Multi Factor Authentication (MFA), no shared IDs, and others.

Requirement #9 is about physical access. If the previous two were about protecting data, this one is about protecting your premises, your offices, your rooms, and your physical storage media. Measures related to cameras, visitor identification, access control to rooms, and more. Requirement #10 is about monitoring. Or, in other words, logging. Having a logging solution, keeping the time synchronization consistent across different logs, backing them up as soon as possible, and a couple of other measures, such as File Integrity Monitoring (FIM) on the logs to prevent tampering. Then, Requirement #11 is about testing regularly.

Doing vulnerability scanning, penetration testing, and other types of measures to prevent intrusions in your network. Then, the final requirement is about having an information security policy across the organization, for people at all levels, related to all aspects, from Incident Responses (IR), to technology use, and more. And finally, the closing topic for this chapter will be a discussion of some general patterns, in the 12 Requirements, as well as a final recap of these. So, as you see, in this chapter, we are going to cover all 12 requirements. We'll start with an introduction of all 12, using the simpler names that I've given them, then we'll cover every single one of them in detail, then we'll summarize all of them once again.

Overview Of The 12 Requirements

Let's cover an overview of the 12 requirements, as of version 3.2.1. That is, before we dive deep, and go into the "second layer" of knowledge, if you will, I want to just give you a "first layer" of knowledge, to tell you a little bit about every single requirement, and what it represents. I've also given a simpler name to each one of these, to make them catchier, and to make them easier to remember. So, let's take a look. The 12 Requirements of the PCI-DSS are, as of version 3.2.1: The first is about installing and maintaining a firewall configuration to protect your card data from traffic. Requirement #2 is about not using defaults. Default passwords, default accounts, and so on, with the purpose of minimizing vulnerabilities.

Requirement #3 is about protecting stored data, with strong encryption and proper key management in your databases. Then, Requirement #4 is about encrypting transmission of sensitive data, especially across public networks. Requirement #5 is about protecting all systems against malware, as well as keeping the antivirus updated. Requirement #6: Develop and maintain secure systems and applications. Including security requirements in your development lifecycle, as well as applying patches in a timely manner. Requirement #7 is about restricting access to sensitive data by need to know. Minimize who has access to the data, and what access every person has.

Requirement #8 is about identifying and authenticating access to system components. Every person has a unique ID, they use strong authentication, and other measures, to make sure that every action is tracked back to the user. Requirement #9 is about restricting physical access. Safely storing and moving physical media, visitor control, and so on. Requirement #10 is about tracking and monitoring all access to networks and data. In other words, logging, logging and more logging!

Requirement #11 is about regular vulnerability and penetration testing of systems and processes. And finally, Requirement #12 is about maintaining a policy, itself, that addresses information security for all personnel.

Now, the original names are a bit complex, so in practice, I've simplified them, and these are the names that I'll use throughout the Book. They help you memorize the requirements with fewer words. I call Requirement #1 "Keep a Firewall". Have proper firewall rules, restrict unknown traffic, have a firewall on all machines, and use change management for changing every firewall rule. The second requirement is "No Defaults". For obvious reasons. Change all default passwords and all accounts, isolate servers - one functionality, or one security level for server - inventory your assets, and remove all unneeded functionality. It's about minimizing obvious vulnerabilities.

Requirement #3 is "Protect Stored Data". It's supposed to contrast with #4, which is "Protect Transmitted Data", as these are a mirror of each other. So Requirement #3 is about limiting the card data that you store to the essentials, properly purging it once you don't need it, masking Personal Account Numbers (PANs) that are written down, or stored, and having proper key encryption and key lifecycle management. Key custodians, a defined cryptoperiod, and so on. Requirement #4, as stated, is "Protect Transmitted Data". Make sure the data are encrypted with strong encryption in transit, including for public wireless networks - such as satellite GPS, GSM, as well as never sending plaintext Personal Account Numbers (PANs).

Then, Requirement #5 is "Prevent Malware". Very simple. Have a proper antivirus software that is regularly updated, that performs regular scans, and that outputs regular logs, and that cannot be disabled by individual users, through establishing a policy. So if Requirement #5 is about protection from vulnerabilities that others cause, #6 is about protecting yourself from the vulnerabilities that YOU cause. It's about developing securely. And it's not just your own applications. It's securing both off-the-shelf software, and your own, with regular risk ranking, and patch installation for critical risks, but also including security requirements in the software development lifecycle (SDLC) and in developer training.

Your developers need to be able to deal with code injections, buffer overflows, cross-site scripting, and more. The next three are related. "Need-to-Know Access", "Identify Access" and "Restrict Physical Access". This is about digital protection. This is about digital identification. And this is about physical protection. So, let's start with #7. Need-to-Know Access. As the name says, it defends the Principle of Least Privilege, or PoLP. Defining user roles, with the least privilege possible to perform a task. If this person can do this with less access, give them less access. If they don't need access at all to card data, then cut it off. And using access control for systems or networks that represents this.

Requirement #8 is simplified as "Identify Access' '. Make sure that there are unique IDs, no shared users, strong authentication, Multi Factor Authentication (MFA), no sharing physical access control devices - so, one person can't use the badge of somebody else - and restricting database access only to administrators. Then, Requirement #9 is about physical access. Entry control to rooms and critical areas, visitor distinction - for example, with color coding - and proper authorization, restricting physical access to rooms, to media, or any place with card data, and having strict policies for media storage - such as databases, or USB pens - distribution policies - so if a hard drive is moved, why is it being moved? And proper training of individuals to identify tampering, for example, with POS devices.

Then, Requirement #9 is simplified as "Monitor Networks", but it could be simplified as "Logging". It's all about logging. Logging specific events - so, any event involving card data is logged. Any action taken by an admin is logged. Any intrusion attempt is long. Every failed operation is logged. And so on. And within those specific events, there's also specific data elements that must be logged. What's the status of the operation? What's the user ID? What's the machine? And so on? Also, having one time synchronization for all log machines, to make sure that you can interpret the logged timestamps, from different machines, in a consistent way, using File Integrity Monitoring (FIM), to make sure that your logs are not tampered with, proper log retention - so, for example, you must keep the last year of logs - and immediate log alert responses, in the case of intrusions, for example.

Requirement # 11 is simplified as "Test Regularly". Doing risk assessments once a year - or more frequently - doing both vulnerability scanning and penetration testing - so, one is more general, just about identifying vulnerabilities, while penetration testing is simulating a real-world attack - and having this done by proper professionals, called ASVs, or Authorized Scan Vendors. Then, doing regular identification of all your Access Points - both the legit ones and the rogue ones - having an Intrusion Detection System (IDS) or Intrusion Prevention System (IPS), and having File Integrity Monitoring (FIM) on all critical files. Not just logs, but other ones, such as, for example, system files. And finally, Requirement #12 is simplified as, have an "Information Security Policy".

It's the only requirement that is not about technology, but management. It can be considered the sum of all policies: usage policies, incident response policies, risk assessment practices, employee screening - including background checks and others - employee roles and responsibilities - including having an owner for everything, and I mean EVERYTHING - every task, every system, every network -

having employee awareness, so, making the policies reach these people - and proper training. Let's go one layer deeper now. And, naturally, each one of the requirements still has its own chapter. But let me tell you a little bit more about each of these. I want to progressively expand on every requirement, so that you can progressively know more about them.

So Requirement #1, "Keep a Firewall", is overall about blocking access to the Card Data Environment (CDE), by having a firewall, but also having clear rules for inbound and outbound traffic. You'll notice the inclusion of outbound traffic. Many firewall admins focus on inbound traffic - protecting themselves from attackers - but what if the attacker is already in your network, and they want to get out with data? So you need to protect yourself from inbound and outbound traffic. It's important to note that two essential documents are the network topology and the card data flows, because these clarify what must be done in terms of firewall configuration. You need the network topology to know what are the junctions that you actually need to protect with a firewall, and you need the card data flows to actually know where the card data passes through. What are the systems and networks in scope of PCI-DSS compliance.

But besides having these rules, it's important to have change management for them as well. For example, you may have the most sophisticated firewall ever, but then John comes and says, "Hey, can you whitelist this domain so that I can go online gambling?", and the firewall admin says, "OK". That's a very big vulnerability, OK? So, there must be a documented process, - and a change management process - for all firewall config changes. Then, Requirement #2 is all about "No Defaults". It's about removing the default passwords, and default accounts, and default standards, to block access to your systems and networks. So, if you have some experience with cyber security, you will know that the default passwords for all types of equipment are online, and anybody can find them.

So you need to patch these vulnerabilities. But besides the passwords, and the defaults, there are other points, such as not storing multiple functionality in one server. I mean, some of them make sense, but some don't. For example, your DNS server and Active Directory server can be in the same server - they're in the same layer - but your application server and DNS server should not be in the same server. This is because, if an attacker compromises a server, you want to have the least amount of functionality there, as well as disabling unnecessary functionality from systems and devices. So if you're installing a new router, you don't just need to change the password. You need to ask yourself, for every port that's open, or every service, "Is there a reason for the service?", and if there isn't, turn it off. It's about minimizing obvious vulnerabilities.

Requirement #3: "Protect Stored Data". It's about, well, protecting stored data! Both in databases, with truncating, tokenizing, encrypting, masking, but also physical media. For example, if you have printed logs with card numbers on them, they better not be the full number. The goal is that, even if the attacker obtains some of your data, that data is garbage. An effective key lifecycle comes in here. So, you must use strong encryption keys to begin with, but you also need to take into account the expiration of the keys (the cryptoperiod) having key custodians, maybe split knowledge, and so on. But also, better than protecting data is to avoid storing those data in the first place.

So, it's about analyzing what you store and minimizing it, as well as properly purging data that you don't need any more. It's not just about protecting the actual data, but it's about minimizing what you store. Because what you don't store doesn't need to be protected. Then, if Requirement #3 was about protecting the STORED data, Requirement #4 is about protecting the TRANSMITTED data. It's simply about maintaining encryption of data when transmitting it. So similarly, it's about using strong encryption. By the way, this is not strong authentication, strong encryption - sorry! For example, using AES 256 or 3DES. It's important to note that this doesn't just include Wi-Fi, but mobile, Bluetooth or any other communication modalities. And in that case, you need a standard such as WPA or WPA2 - never WEP, for example.

Strong encryption is mandatory. And the requirement itself dictates some good standards for this protection, like the FIPS or OWASP ones. And there is a specific sub-requirement about never sending Personal Account Numbers (PANs) as plaintext. In other words, sending a full credit card number via instant message, or email. Never. Always masking them, or encrypting them, or some other mechanism. Remember, if an attacker gets the data, they must be garbage. Then, Requirement #5 is deceptively simple. "Prevent Malware". So you must have an antivirus solution, that is frequently updated, to keep up with new malware, as well as regular scans that are executed, and the logs must be retained.

It's also important that there should be an access control policy, so that an individual user can't just disable the antivirus. Because that would be a very big vulnerability! As we'll see, there can be exceptions... but they're exceptions for a reason. Requirement #6, "Developing Securely", is all about mitigating vulnerabilities in developed applications. And off-the-shelf ones as well. It's about having a secure software development lifecycle (SDLC), as well as applying patches - both for your applications and off-the-shelf ones - in a timely manner. Critical patches within 1 month. And other patches within 2 to 3 months. This is usually one of the hardest requirements to achieve, and for a very funny reason, which is that most developers don't care about security.

They want to code features. They're excited by features. So they have to be trained in terms of how to avoid all common vulnerabilities, from cross-site scripting (XSS), to buffer overflows, and do this for every single application that is developed. And every single version that is released. And, besides the initial deployment of applications, changes to these must also be managed. With rollback policies, in case of problematic changes, and so on. Requirement #7, "Need-to-Know Access", is all about restrictive access control. And I mean both digital and physical. It's based on something called the Principle of Least Privilege (PoLP): the least permissions possible for a user to perform something.

If possible, no permissions! So take any employee. If they can perform their job function by not knowing the full Personal Account Number (PAN), but just a masked version, such as the 6 first digits, and the last 4, then reduce what they have access to. Or can they even do their whole job without access to card data at all? Then remove it. That's the logic. This minimizes access to Cardholder Data (CHD) by users. And naturally, any changes to roles, and their permissions, must be managed through a formal change management process. Requirement #8, "Identifying Access", is all about non-repudiation and accountability. In other words, if something happens, you want to identify the human point of failure.

You don't want a situation, for example, where a vulnerability was exposed by your general "guest" account, or "admin" account, but you do want a situation where it was exposed by your employee David, for example, and that he used Multi Factor Authentication (MFA) to log in. So you really know it was him. That's what this requirement is about. So it includes sub-requirements such as unique user IDs, no group users, no shared users, and properly removing old employees. It also includes other measures, such as strong password practices, locking up someone's account, on a certain number of failed attempts and automatic logouts after a period of inactivity, such as 15 minutes. It also includes the usage of strong authentication measures that are unique to the person. So Multifactor Authentication (MFA), fobs, smart cards, badges, and so on.

To make sure that it's really this person. Requirement, #9 is about restricting physical access. It's the real-world equivalent of requirement #7. Requirement #7 was about limiting digital access. And this one is about limiting physical access. Both to devices and people. It's about CCTV, locked rooms, safes, restricted areas and more. The goal is to prevent attackers from both tampering with your devices - using keyloggers, or placing skimmers on your POS devices - or tampering with your people - by using social engineering. It also includes procedures for safe storage of media, safe transportation, and safe disposal.

So if you have a hard drive, with Cardholder Data (CHD), how secure is it? What are the rules for transporting it, especially outside the premises? And when disposed of, do you have the certificate for that? And so on. Requirement #10 is about "Monitoring Networks", or, in simpler terms, It's about constant logging. If an attack occurs, you want to know when and you want to know where. There are specific elements of data that must be stored for each log entry, such as the user, the type of operation, and so on - as well as specific events that always must be logged - including all intrusion attempts, all admin actions, all operations with Cardholder Data (CHD), and more. The time for these logs must be synchronized using one mechanism.

This is to facilitate interpretation of chains of events across different machines - because if they're off by even one minute, it's going to be very confusing to reconcile those logs! It also includes the usage of FIM - or File Integrity Management - solutions, because attackers change logs. So, it's crucial to know if that occurred. Logs should also be backed up in a secure location, as close to real time as possible, to prevent tampering to begin with. Requirement #11 is about "Testing Regularly", both your networks and your systems, to identify vulnerabilities and prevent attacks. This means, for example, performing both internal and external tests.

For example, doing an audit of all Access Points (APs), both legitimate and rogue ones, or, for example, doing a periodic audit of all IP addresses in your network, and seeing how they changed since last time. It also includes both vulnerability scanning and penetration testing. So, vulnerability scanning will be more general, and will just tell you your weak points, while penetration testing is much more hands-on, and specific to the company, and will simulate a real attack. It's important to note that the assessor for these scans must be qualified, which is what the PCI-DSS defines as an ASV, or Approved Scanning Vendor. And here's the key. They can be someone internal or external to your company.

As long as they are qualified. And finally, Requirement #12, about an Information Security policy, is the only requirement that's not about technology, but management. It's about having pervasive controls at all levels. Seriously! It touches all roles, all systems, and all levels that deal with Cardholder Data (CHD). It includes, for example, technology usage policies. What technology can be used, what type of server, what type of operating system, what type of antivirus software. What's the acceptable use for those computers and servers? So, for example, telling employees that they can't read pirated movies on company computers, as well as having rules for that selection. And also, naturally, managing those assets.

It also includes, for example, employee screening - having yearly background checks and NDAs on Cardholder Data (CHD). And one of the most important points is having incident management procedures. Incident Response (IR). So having people available 24/7, having a process, having a clear set of actions - and testing these yearly, not just having them on paper! These 12 requirements can seem complex to tackle, and we'll take a look at each one of them, in detail, in their own chapter. But in order to simplify things even more, I use a personal mnemonic of 4 statements starting with "Keep It", that simplify them. So, for example, each requirement is either about keeping it locked, keeping it blocked, keeping it identified, or keeping it updated. So all of the 12 requirements will fit, in some way, this mnemonic.

So keeping it locked is about preventing access. Having safe, encrypted, secure data, secure media, isolated physical locations, and so on. It's literally locked, so it can't be accessed. Keeping it blocked is about blocking vulnerabilities, blocking access to traffic, blocking unauthorized access, blocking malware, and so on. The attacker can't reach it. Keeping it identified is about identifying accesses and users. Knowing who did what, in all types of systems. And keeping it updated is about making sure that you are up to date on protection. Keeping systems updated, keeping antivirus updated, keeping risk assessment updated, keeping your software tests updated - in terms of development - keeping your vulnerability testing updated, keeping your logs updated, and so on.

So, we can easily match each requirement to this mnemonic. In fact, some requirements could certainly be more than one. So, #1, keep a firewall. Definitely keep it blocked! Blocking traffic. Requirement #2, about no default, is keeping it blocked as well. Blocking vulnerabilities and exploits. Requirement #3, "Protect stored Data", is about keeping it locked, Making sure the data is locked, digitally. Requirement #4 keep it locked. For the same reason. The data can't be accessed. Requirement #5, "Prevent Malware", is about keeping it blocked. Blocking malware and viruses. Requirement #6, "Develop Securely", is about keeping it blocked. Blocking vulnerabilities and exploits, specifically, those that your developers may be causing themselves! Requirement #7, "Need-to-Know Access", is about keeping it blocked.

Blocking access from roles that don't have permission. Requirement #8, "Identify Access", is keeping it identified. Knowing exactly who is doing what in your systems. Requirement #9, "Restricting Physical Access", is keeping it blocked. Blocking physical access to your premises and data. Requirement #10, "Monitoring Networks", is about keeping it identified. Identifying actions, events, timestamps. Requirement #11, "Testing Regularly", is about keeping it updated. Being updated on risk assessment, vulnerability auditing and test results.

You could argue that it should be "Keep it blocked", because you're blocking access from attackers. But I think the most important component of this requirement is doing it frequently. Because a vulnerability scan from two years ago is not going to help you! And, finally, Requirement #12, about an Information Security policy, is about keeping it identified. Identifying owners, roles, responsibilities, users, for every area of the organization. Just to close the chapter, out of curiosity, there are 6 goals in PCI-DSS (At least, as of version 3.2.1). And, in this Book, we are going to focus on the requirements and not the goals. But let me just illustrate the relationship between them in a minute. So Goal #1 is to "Build and Maintain a Secure Network and Systems". And this includes 2 requirements.

Requirement #1, about keeping a firewall, and Requirement #2, about not having defaults in your system. Goal #2 is about "Protecting Cardholder Data", and it includes Requirements #3, about "Protecting Stored Data", and Requirement #4, about "Protecting Transmitted Data". Goal #3 is about "Maintaining a Vulnerability Management Program", and this both includes Requirement #5, so, "No Malware", and Requirement #6, "Develop Securely". So, no vulnerabilities from viruses, and no vulnerabilities from your own applications. Goal #4 is about "Implementing Strong Access Control Measures", and it includes 3 requirements. Requirement #7 is about "Need-to-Know Access".

Requirement #8 is about "Identifying Access" - unique IDs and so on - while Requirement #9 is about "Restricting Physical Access". Then, goal #5 is about "Regularly Monitoring and Testing Networks". And this includes Requirement #10, "Monitor Networks", which is about logging, as well as Requirement #11, "Test Regularly", which is about vulnerability scanning, penetration testing and intrusion prevention. And finally, the last goal is to "Maintain an Information Security Policy", and it's only requirement has pretty much the same name! Having an Information Security policy across the whole organization.

What are some examples? The first is that we will have policies everywhere! You will notice this as we examine the different requirements, but one of the most pervasive elements is having policies. Policies to update the anti-virus, policies for secure development, policies for access control, and more. In every requirement, you will see that the last sub-requirements says, "Document and enforce these procedures". Then, minimizing scope. One of the most important things that an organization can do is to minimize the scope of their Card Data Environment (CDE). Remember, the organization must only comply with the PCI-DSS in terms of the Card Data Environment.

So, the more that organizations can reduce the scope of the CDE, the less work they will have, because the less they have to comply with. Then, as you're probably guessing, the PCI-DSS are very comprehensive and full. They are a true cybersecurity tour de force. They impose checks on physical and logical access, on system and network security, data management, encryption key management, and many other areas. What are our key takeaways here? The first is that the 12 requirements of the PCI-DSS framework cover all areas of cybersecurity, from vulnerability scanning and protection, to data encryption, to access control, and more! Then, many of the requirements are related and complementary.

They mirror each other. For example, requirements #3 and #4. Protect Stored Data and Protect Transmitted Data. Or, Requirements #7 and #9. Restrict logical access and restrict physical access. Among others. And finally, keep in mind the 4 "Keep It"s mnemonic. This can help in memorizing every requirement. So, each requirement either keeps it blocked, keeps it locked, keeps it identified, or keeps it updated. So, as you see, these are the 12 requirements of the PCI-DSS. Many of them are complementary - or even overlap, in certain areas - but that is understandable, because the PCI-DSS are a true cybersecurity tour de force. They cover every single area that you may think of!

Requirement 1: Keep a Firewall

Let's talk about Requirement #1, which I gave the simplified name of "Keep a Firewall". As you may be thinking, it is about blocking connections, and blocking traffic. But it's more than that. It's about having sophistication in how you deal with the firewall itself. Configuration management, no direct access to configuration files, and many other measures to not only have a firewall, but have it be advanced and sophisticated. Let's take a look. Let's talk about Requirement #1 - Installing and Maintaining a Firewall Configuration. Or "Keep a Firewall", in the simplified name. This requirement is all about protecting your Card Data Environment from traffic, and I mean both inbound and outbound.

It may be an attacker trying to get in, which is inbound traffic, but also an attacker that's already in your system trying to get out with the data, which would be outbound traffic. But the key here is that it's not just about running a firewall, but also having proper change management for changes, as well as keeping documentation of your network topology and your card data flows. This requirement has 5 major sub-requirements, which we'll take a look at in detail, and which are: First, setting configuration standards. Firewall rules. Then, restricting connections between untrusted networks, or, in other words, denying unauthorized traffic. 1.3 is about prohibiting direct access from the Internet to the Card Data Environment.

You need to have an intermediary space, called the DMZ, where all incoming traffic is redirected to for triage. And only then may it go to the CDE. Then 1.4 is about installing firewall software on all computers accessing the Card Data Environment. And 1.5 is about documenting and enforcing all of these policies and procedures. Not just doing it, but doing it formally. So let's start with sub-requirement

1.1. It's about setting configuration standards. That is, having standards for traffic configurations, for security protocols, and rules related to the firewall. And when it says "having standards", you don't need to have specific rules, or specific roles.

You just need to have a process to define these. It's important to note that both the network topology and the card data flows must be documented. This is essential to the configuration standards. If you don't know where data is going, you can't protect it. You must also establish something a DMZ, and this comes from a military term, which is a Demilitarized Zone. It's kind of a neutral zone between your military forces and the enemy. And the purpose here is exactly the same. It's a zone that separates your local networks - your forces - and the enemy - which is the Internet. So this is kind of a triage area for traffic. It's the neutral terrain between your local networks and the untrusted traffic.

Then, there must be a change management process for configurations. This means a person can't just come and request that the firewall admin whitelists a domain and get it like that. There must be a formal form for these. And, finally, there must be regular reviews - usually, every 6 months - of these procedures and configurations, because technology changes and attacks change. Sub-requirement 1.2 is about restricting connections between untrusted networks. In simple terms, it's about preventing all external untrusted traffic. It's isolating the CDE, having a logic of denying everything that you don't trust, by nature.

So, this includes limiting both inbound and outbound traffic to and from the CDE. It also includes, by the way, securely storing the router configuration files, so that they can't be tampered with. That would be a way to manipulate your firewall without actually manipulating the firewall itself. And it also includes positioning firewalls between all wireless networks in Card Data Environment (CDE) traffic. So at any juncture where your card data environment is accessed, there must be a firewall. Period. If you have 50 Wi-Fi networks that access the CDE, if 49 of them have a firewall and one of them doesn't, you fail to comply.

This is why, again, documents like the network topology and the card data flows are so important. Because, if you don't have those, you don't know which junctures must be protected with a firewall. Requirement 1.3 is about prohibiting public, direct, access from the internet to the CDE. It's pretty self-explanatory. You don't want public traffic from the Internet being able to reach your Cardholder Data (CHD), period. So this involves creating that DMZ to limit the inbound traffic. So, the inbound traffic goes to this neutral zone first, instead of going directly to the Card Data Environment, and the DMZ triages it and decides whether it proceeds to the CDE, or not.

It also includes using anti-spoofing measures, to prevent spoofed IPs from entering the Card Data Environment itself. And again, it mandates no direct traffic from the Internet to the card data environment. It must be triaged first. And it also mandates that all card data devices must be in local isolated networks. In other words, you can't isolate your card data from the internet if the device itself is connected to the internet! So, these devices must be in local networks that only connect to the internet using the DMZ. No exceptions, never directly. Then, requirement 1.4 is about installing firewall software on all portable computers that access the CDE.

As the name says, all portable computers must use a firewall. This prevents vulnerabilities from individual computers. In other words, you may have 50 networks, and 50 servers, that are all completely safe, but it only takes one employee, with one laptop that doesn't have a firewall, to let an intruder in. So, every laptop must be secured as well. And here's the thing: All those settings cannot always be standardized, especially if different laptops have different operating systems and different versions of software. They may need to be customized. That's fine. But the key here is that individual users may never be able to change their settings.

One user can't just turn off their firewall because they want a faster connection, for example. If they want a change, they need to submit it through a formal change management process. The goal here is to minimize the vulnerabilities from specific laptops. Then finally, sub-requirement 1.5 is to document and enforce all policies and procedures. And we will see this one at the end of every one of the 12 requirements. What this requirement says, pretty much, is that staff must know - and follow! - the security policies and procedures established here. So what they do can't just be ad hoc. It must be a formal process. So, producing the network topology documents, restricting unauthorized traffic, having firewalls on all computers...

that must be a set of policies and procedures that are written down, and that people must comply with formally. So, essentially, it's about staff training. It's about making sure that your employees that deal with equipment that is vulnerable to internet traffic - both firewall admins, and just the laptop users - know the procedures to avoid vulnerabilities. What are some examples here? The first is that documents should be rigorous. The more rigorous that the network topology and the card data flowchart are, the less vulnerabilities will go unnoticed, and the more protected the CDE is. Another point, already mentioned, is to keep in mind outbound traffic.

A lot of firewall admins focus just on the inbound traffic to prevent external attackers. But they should also focus on outbound traffic, because there may be an attacker already in your system, trying to exfiltrate data. And finally, this requirement shares one principle in common with a lot of other requirements, which is "deny by nature". In this case, deny traffic by nature. If there's no justification for a service or open port, block it. If there's no justification for a specific type of traffic, block it. And so on. Deny everything by nature. What are our key takeaways here? The first is that this requirement is essentially about keeping a firewall.

Restrict traffic, isolate the Card Data Environment from the internet, and make sure that documentation and processes support this. Then, sub-requirement 1 is about setting standards. Have documentation, including network topology and card data flows, have a change management process, and ensure the frequent review of these. Sub-requirement 1.2 is about restricting traffic. Restrict traffic from untrusted networks, and position firewalls between all networks that are adjacent to the Card Data Environment (CDE). In other words, don't let the Card Data Environment touch anything without protection, in terms of networks, and store the configuration files securely.

Requirement 1.3 is about no direct access. So, prevent unsecured traffic from public sources, and for this, use the DMZ as an intermediary, as well as minimizing open ports and vulnerabilities, as well as unneeded traffic. 1.4 is about enforcing firewall usage on all portable computers, because these are especially vulnerable, and they must be protected. And also, not letting users change that. And 1.5, finally, is about documenting and enforcing all policies and standards. So, employees must know what these procedures are, and they must put them to work. The standards, the connection restriction, direct traffic prevention, firewall on all PCs...

this must all be on paper. And employees must use it. So, as we see, Requirement #1 is about keeping a firewall. It is about having a DMZ, isolating unsecured traffic, having traffic rules, and more, but it's also about documentation, about safety practices, about access control, and more. In short, it's not just about having a firewall, but treating it in a sophisticated manner.

Requirement 2: No Defaults

Let's talk about Requirement #2, which I gave the simplified name of "No Defaults". As you may be thinking, it is about changing the default settings, or default passwords, and so on - because, in most cases, they are public knowledge for any model of a certain system - but the message goes beyond it. It's also about patching stupid mistakes and obvious vulnerabilities. So, the philosophy of "No Defaults" is about preventing problems which are very obvious. Let's take a look at this requirement in more detail. Requirement #2, with the full name of, "Do not use vendor-supplied defaults for system passwords and security parameters", or the simplified name of, "No Defaults", is all about minimizing vulnerabilities, by eliminating the obvious ones.

What I mean is that, nowadays, you can type the name of any system, any router, any operating system, and you will get the default passwords for it, with a Google search, in less than five seconds! So, you must assume that all attackers will leverage this, and you must plug these leaks accordingly. It's not just about changing the defaults, but also removing functionality, removing systems, applications, open ports, or any other element that's not needed - and is just waiting to become a vulnerability. This requirement has 6 sub-requirements, in itself. The first is to always change all default passwords, accounts, connection strings, and so on. Or, if you can't change them, disable them.

Then, 2.2 is about setting configuration standards that address all those vulnerabilities. 2.3 is about encrypting all admin access. Even if you change the password, the connection can still be unsecured. And you don't want a man in the middle to intercept your admin credentials. 2.4 is about inventorying all assets that are in scope of PCI-DSS. And we'll take a look at this one, naturally, in more detail, but out of curiosity, it's not about the inventory. It's just a signal. Because managers that inventory their assets are more likely to protect them. So that's what the assessor is looking at. Then, 2.5 is our usual "document and enforce policies and procedures".

So, all these 4 points must not be done ad hoc, but formally, as processes that employees know about and enforce. And, then, 2.6 is a requirement just for service providers, and it's a requirement to isolate their multitenant clients. So, if you have a shared hosting space, you have to make sure that your scripts, your applications, and so on, do not let one client access the data of other clients. The first sub-requirement, 2.1, is about always changing all defaults. Or disabling the accounts. And please notice here that it's not just changing default passwords, but also default account names - such as "admin" or "guest" - default encryption keys, default connection strings, and so on.

For every piece of equipment that you purchase, there will be a set of defaults, and you need to make sure that those defaults are changed, in every single case! Again, consider that all defaults are public, on the internet, and attackers will be able to find them - very quickly! And again, this should be in procedures. I'm not talking about just casually changing the passwords, when you buy something. It's about having a formal process with a checklist. "Change this when deploying this type of equipment", or "What is the formal process for a new server instance?", for example. Sub-requirement 2.2 is about having configuration standards that address all vulnerabilities. This is about setting standards when installing or deploying.

It's not just changing the defaults, but, also, separating or removing functionality. Let me elaborate. For example, you want to have one function per server - or, at least, all the functions just of one level of security. For example, it would be acceptable to have your Active Directory (AD) and DNS on the same server - because they're on the same layer - but not, for example, your Active Directory and your web-facing application. So, the goal here is to group functionality per security level - or, if you can, the holy grail is to have one function per server. This is because, if an attacker compromises a server, they only compromise one service. And you can do this with real servers, if you have the capital - or with virtualization, if you don't.

Another point is removing all vulnerable functions, or setting additional measures. This can be as obvious as detecting that a certain device has an open Telnet port and immediately disabling it - or it can be more subtle, such as a device that has a protocol, that is secure, but that's possibly not needed, and that can be removed, or replaced with another protocol that's always secure. Or, in case you can't remove something that is vulnerable, because you need it, making it secure. For example, the telnet service is not necessarily a deal breaker. If you just use it by itself, it IS a deal breaker! But if you can wrap it, for example, in TLS, or SSL, in every instance, then it may become acceptable. Next, 2.3. Encrypting all admin access.

This is to minimize the chances that an attacker can sniff the admin credentials, if they're already in the network. So, if they are in the network, sniffing packets, if access is encrypted, they'll get nothing. So, first, plaintext protocols like Telnet or HTTP should never be used. And the major offender in this case are usually your own developed apps! So, imagine this. All firewalls and routers and servers have secure admin login. But you have an admin backend webpage, that your own company developed, where you log in through HTTP, and you do it. And now, the attacker has your login - and the point of failure was you. Out of curiosity, that's why Requirement #6, "Develop Securely", is so important.

So this is why all admin access, for every server, or app, must be done using strong cryptography. Using NIST standards, or the FIPS standard, or OWASP standards, and so on. 2.4 is doing an inventory of all assets in scope of PCI-DSS. As the name says, it's doing an audit of all devices that deal with Cardholder Data (CHD). And again, this measure is actually more of an indicator. The assessor is not looking to know how sophisticated your excel sheet, or inventory management system is. This is a signal - because companies that don't know what assets they have are probably not protecting them! So, this can be done in multiple ways - and Excel is acceptable - but an automated tool is even better, because it allows for change management processes.

If possible, this asset list should be run against a port scan. In other words, trying to match each open port to a specific device. The assessor will do this, and you should be doing it yourself. And, finally, it should not be a static inventory list, but updated with a change management process. If a new device is installed, is the port scan updated? Are the ports mapped to the devices? Or does this not even enter the process? 2.5 is our usual requirement of documenting and enforcing the policies and procedures. So, if all the previous points were about making sure that you have procedures to mitigate vulnerabilities - either by removing them, or by adding protective measures - then, this point is about making sure that your workforce knows about these procedures, and that they put them to use.

So it's a formal process. Then, 2.6 is the conditional sub-requirement, in case you are a service provider. Specifically, a shared service provider. And the sub-requirement is about making sure that you comply with the PCI-DSS Appendix A1. And this is an appendix, beyond the 12 requirements, that is just for shared service providers. And all of the measures in this appendix are to make sure that any scripts, or any devices, or any applications that you have, that can access data of other tenants are especially protected. For example, how many times have you used a website that was just created, by a startup, for example, and you could view your ID - for example, you go to a website.

com/profile/id/36, if you were 36, and then, out of curiosity, you change the 36 to a 35, and you find out that you can access somebody else's private profile data! So, this is exactly what we DON'T want to happen! It's about making sure that there are no vulnerabilities that allow one client of yours, as a service provider, to access the data of another client. What are some examples here? The first are security levels. In servers, specifically. Although the ideal is one functionality per server - so, one server for DNS, one server for a web application, one server for Active Directory - which would provide perfect isolation - if you can't achieve that, the second best case scenario is grouping functions with similar security levels.

For example, you can't have the database and Active Directory in the same server, but Active Directory and DNS are fine, because they're part of the same layer. Then, remember the inventory as a proxy. Although asset inventorying is important, in this case, the focus is not on the asset inventory itself - by the way, the focus is NOT on the inventory. Sorry, I ended up typing the opposite. The focus is NOT on the inventory, it's a signal. If you know what assets you have, you're likely protecting them. If you read the book Freakonomics, where they talked about the Van Halen list of requirements for their concerts, you know the story about the Brown M&Ms, where they would request the venue to have a bowl with M&Ms, and the brown ones removed.

And here's the key - they didn't care about the M&Ms, but they knew that if a venue took care of the M&Ms, they read the list of requirements, to a deep level, and they took care of all the technical configurations - for the sound, and etc. And they knew that, if they reached a venue, and they didn't take out the brown M&Ms - or didn't even have the M&Ms! - they did not take care of everything else. So, they were a signal. The same exact logic applies here. And, finally, a great way to think about admin access encryption is to think, "What if an attacker already got in the network?". And this mindset is very useful for a lot of the requirements! If you assume that you already have a sleeper attacker in your network, you can think of how to protect yourself from the inside.

What are our key takeaways for Requirement #2? The first is no defaults. Requirement #2 is mostly about removing vulnerabilities. Removing OBVIOUS vulnerabilities. Removing everything that's unnecessary or not secured. Or, if you can't remove it, at least protect it further! 2.1, in specific, is very basic. Change the defaults. Default passwords, default connection strings, default account names, default scripts, default encryption keys, and so on. Don't have anything that a hacker can publicly access with a Google search.

Then, 2.2 is about addressing vulnerabilities. Everything that is installed, or deployed, should have a procedure that specifically removes its vulnerabilities, or, on the other hand, protects them until they're not vulnerable anymore. If there's a router that has an open telnet port, you must have a procedure for every installation of such a router. Disable the telnet port - or secure it. And this must be a formal procedure. Sub-requirement 2.3 is about admin access encryption. Specifically, encrypting all admin access in your internal networks, so, in the case of an intruder invading the network, they can't sniff the admin credentials by sniffing the traffic. So, no plaintext protocols, plus strong encryption, that can't be cracked easily. Then, 2.4 is about inventorying the assets. Inventorying all devices in scope of PCI-DSS. Remember, the goal is not the inventory, but a signal.

If you know what you have, you're probably protecting it. Then, finally, 2.5 and 2.6. 2.5 is our usual "document and enforce" sub-requirement. All these four previous points must be formal policies and procedures on paper. Not done casually. Then, 2.6 is specific to shared service providers, and it's about securing the shared functions. You want to isolate the data of each client, so that no script, or app, or service causes cross-contamination. So, as we see, this requirement is not just about changing the defaults - although it also is about that - but also, about removing any vulnerabilities which may be obvious, or very stupid. So, removing functionality which is not needed, encrypting admin access, and more.

Requirement 3: Protect Stored Data

Let's talk about Requirement #3, which has the simplified name of "Protect Stored Data". And, as the name says, it's about protecting data which are at rest, in databases, in files, and so on. Not in transit. But it's not just about encrypting them, but possibly using other methods, such as masking - or at least, not being in plaintext! - but also, other activities, such as, for example, key management. Let's take a look. Requirement #3, with the official name of, "Protect stored Cardholder Data", is very straightforward, and it's all about making sure that your stored Cardholder Data is properly protected. It's about both making sure that the encryption used is strong by nature, but that it's also properly managed itself.

For example, with proper key management and key lifecycle. It's also about protecting the Personal Account Number (PAN) stored. Remember, stored data is not just digital data. They're also receipts on paper, logs on paper, or any other medium that contains Cardholder Data (CHD). Sub-requirements of Requirement #3 include: First, limiting the storage and retention of card data to the essential. The most secure way to store data is to never have to store it in the first place! Then, not storing Sensitive Authentication Data (SAD) - such as the CVV number, or the PIN. Period. Then, 3.3, is about masking stored Personal Account Numbers (PANs).

Usually, you can show the first 6 digits - also known as the BIN number, or Bank Identification Number, because these are related to the bank that issued that card - as well as the last 4. Everything else in the middle, that's hidden, is the unique part. If you've ever obtained a receipt, for example, at a restaurant, and the credit card number is shown, but you just see a lot of asterisks in the middle, and you see the first 6 digits and the last 4, this is PCI-DSS at play. Then, 3.4 is rendering the Personal

Account Numbers (PANs) unreadable on all communication channels. Encrypting it, masking it, etc.

Just making sure that, if an attacker intercepts your communication, they can't read the numbers. 3.5 is about procedures for key protection. The keys used to encrypt the card data. And 3.6 is about procedures to manage those keys. The cryptoperiod, having a key custodian, maybe split knowledge, and so on. And finally, 3.7 is the customary "document and enforce" all of these policies and procedures. So, all of these points must not be done informally, but instead with written-down policies that are put into practice. So, first comes requirement 3.1. Cardholder Data (CHD) must be limited in terms of what is stored and what is retained.

And note that this process covers both logical and physical Cardholder Data (CHD). So both databases, but also paper receipts or copies that contain card numbers. And it also covers for how long it may be kept, and how it's disposed of. So, first, you need a data retention policy. What data is kept, and for how long. And this must be what happens in reality. It's not worth it to have a policy that says you store numbers for 30 days, if in practice, they are in the database for years, which is why you also need to clarify how the deletion is done. So printed data can be shredded or burned, and digital data, such as hard drives, can be securely deleted by zeroing out the deleted data - or in the case of physical destruction, they can be demagnetized, shredded or others.

But the key here is: Use common sense. Have a procedure And this policy must be frequently reviewed, at least quarterly. As with many other things, this is because technology changes, your infrastructure changes, and your data retention policy needs to keep up with those. 3.2 is very simple: No storing Sensitive Authentication Data (SAD). Period. Remember. What's usually on the back of the card, such as the CVV code, or the magnetic track, or the PIN number, should never be stored. It's not needed. It can be transmitted, naturally, but it is immediately deleted afterwards. You will notice that with a retailer, like Amazon, when you add your credit card number, it asks you for the number and expiration date.

But it doesn't ask you for the CVV. And then, when you go to pay, it asks you for the CVV, in real time. Unlike the rest of the data, Sensitive Authentication Data (SAD) are never stored. Just used at the moment. But now here's the key: You can't just say that you don't store it. You have to prove that you don't. The responsibility is on you. So by default, you fail, and you have to prove that you pass. And you do this by assessing all possible points in your card data process, where you could acquire Sensitive Authentication Data (SAD), and proving that you don't store it at any of those points. So you have to show the assessor, "This is where we store the card data on our website. And please note that we don't store it here". "Now, here's the part of the flow where they pay, and they input the SAD.

And we also don't store it at this juncture". And you have to do that for every possible point. And this includes storing it in the database, possibly showing it in digital media, printing it, or any other medium. You have to prove that, for every situation where you COULD store this data, that you DON'T store it. Sub-requirement 3.3 is about masking the stored Personal Account Numbers (PANs). Again, first 6 digits and last 4. So you need to inventory all users that could access Cardholder Data, and gauge what every single one of them sees. You usually don't do this by individual user, but by roles - but you still need to do it.

We will cover this in more detail in Requirement #7, about need-to-know access, but there is a principle that's shared here, which is the PoLP - the Principle of Least Privilege. Whatever data the person needs to see to do their job should be the LEAST data possible. So, for any individual that does not need to see the full card number - the Personal Account Number (PAN) - and this is most people, by the way! - they must only see the first 6 digits + the last 4 digits. So call centers support people, people who operate the POS, and many others. In many organizations, this will actually be every single person except the database admin, and the data can even be encrypted in the database.

So even them may not see the full card numbers. Then, 3.4 is about rendering the Personal Account Numbers (PANs) unreadable on all communication channels. This is in case an attacker intercepts your communication. For example, they intercept an email from an employee, who processed a payment, who is communicating a card number to their superior. In these cases, the card data must be unreadable, and there are a myriad means to perform this. You can encrypt it as well, in these mediums. You can mask it. You can tokenize it. You can hash it. All of these are possible. The only key principle is that, if an attacker intercepts the communication, the data is useless! So plaintext data should never, ever, EVER be stored. And I don't just mean digital.

This can be on paper. Look, it can be something as innocent as one employee, noting down a full card number on paper, or having it in an Excel file. This is enough to immediately fail this requirement. Again, this is why we have that sub-requirement of documenting and enforcing these procedures for every single personnel member. 3.5 is about having procedures for encryption key protection. Here's the thing: You may have the strongest encryption on Earth for your database. But if the attacker accesses your keys... you're done. They get the keys to the kingdom. So, besides protecting the data, you have to protect the keys that protect the data.

So this includes documenting your key policy, access control to keys, key backups and more. Also, you should have a policy of storing the keys in the fewest possible places, and accessed by the fewest possible people. You're probably noticing that this is a recurring topic, right? Deny everything by default, and give the least amount of access. It's similar to what we did in Requirement #2, where we minimized the running services, or the ports, or the apps. Same here. Minimize the places where keys are. Every place where the keys are must have a reason. So for example, if you have the keys in 2 places, and you say that you don't want to minimize it, because it's for security - for example, Disaster Recovery (DR) reasons - that's fair. As long as you have a reason for that number.

Then, 3.6 is about having procedures for encryption key management. So, key storage, rotation, transmission, and others. If the previous point was about protecting the keys, this point is about managing them. So first, safe storage and distribution of all keys. That's a "must". Both physical and digital. Then, you should have best practice protocols for defining the cryptoperiod, and for how to deal with expired keys, weakened keys, or compromised keys. Because any, and all, of these may trigger replacement protocols. You can also have split knowledge and dual protocols to minimize damage, in case one person is compromised. So you always need two different people, which minimizes vulnerabilities. And finally, 3.7 is our old friend. The usual "document and enforce policies and procedures" sub-requirement.

As with previous requirements, this is just about making sure that employees are aware of these policies and actually put them to work. How keys are stored. How keys are replaced. How to mask Personal Account Numbers (PANs). And so on. What are some examples? The first is an unexpected way in which you fail compliance, and that is if you have clients that send you, for example, via email, their Personal Account Numbers (PANs). Even worse, if they also send you their Sensitive Authentication Data (SAD). It may not be your fault, but you immediately fail PCI-DSS. You need a process to prevent your clients from doing this as well. Naturally, this is an edge case, but it does happen.

Remember, if full credit card data, in plaintext, arrives at your system, you fail - It doesn't matter where it came from! Then, there are security sub-requirements for both the data and the keys. They're kind of mirrored. If you think about it, all sub-requirements up to 3.4 are about securing the data itself. Then, all requirements from 3.5 onwards are about securing the keys themselves. So, you have to protect the data and protect the keys. And, finally, having a strong reason is a common pattern. This is a pattern that will come up frequently in other requirements. The criteria used to define the cryptoperiod, to manage the keys, and other procedures doesn't need to have specific values. It just needs to have a reason. Common sense.

So that you can show the assessor that you've actually thought about this beforehand. If you say that your cryptoperiod is 2 months, because it matches the replacement of a certain technology, or the timing of your purging processes, that's a good reason. If you say that it's 2 months "just because", you fail to comply! So again, have a good reason. What are our key takeaways here? The first is about protecting Cardholder Data (CHD). It's what this requirement is about. Protect these data in storage, as well as the keys that are used for its encryption. Sub-requirement 3.1 is about limiting storage.

Data retention policies. Explicitly show where Cardholder Data are stored, for how long, and why. And show that it's properly purged through some mechanism. Physically or digitally. And, naturally, don't store the data that you don't need! 3.2 is very simple. Don't store Sensitive Authentication Data (SAD), period. PIN, chip, magnetic track, are all off the table. You also have to show every single point where you COULD store it, and show that you DON'T store it. 3.3 and 3.4 are the following: 3.3 is about masking the data in all mediums that it's stored in. Paper, Excel, database, emails, others. 3.4 is about not letting it be readable, when they're sent in plaintext. If you have receipts, logs or others, at least make sure to mask the data so that it can't be readable if someone intercepts it.

3.5 is about protecting keys, while 3.6 is about managing them. So 3.5 is about minimizing the places where keys are stored, backing them up, and minimizing the amount of people that have access to them. 3.6 is about your practices in terms of managing the keys. Lifecycle, cryptoperiod, key replacement, dual knowledge and so on. And finally, 3.7 is our old friend. Document and enforce. So, all of these sub-requirements that come before cannot be done informally. There must be procedures and policies that are known and enforced by employees. So, as we see, Requirement #3 is about protecting stored data, but it's about doing it in a sophisticated manner. That is, the protection of the data must be protected itself.

Requirement 4: Protect Transmitted

Let's talk about Requirement #4, with the simplified name of "Protect Transmitted Data". If the previous requirement was about protecting data at rest, this one is about protecting them in transit. What to do when you transmit data across WiFi, across other protocols, how should it be protected, and more. Let's take a look! Requirement #4, with the full name of "Encrypt transmission of Cardholder Data across open and public networks" is a counterpart of Requirement #3. So, while the previous one was about protecting stored data, this one is about protecting transmitted data. It's about security in motion. So, you want to keep CHD secure while you transmit it across public networks, and you want to use best practices in terms of encryption to achieve this.

It also deals with the internal transmission of Personal Account Numbers (PANs) in instant message and email. This is a relatively short requirement. You're probably thinking, "Finally", right? It just tells you to, number one, use strong encryption and security in public networks. A standard such as a NIST, FIPS or OWASP one. Then, never send unprotected Personal Account Numbers (PANs) in instant messaging or email. And, finally, document and enforce these policies and procedures. That's it. In higher detail, sub-requirement 4.1 is about using strong encryption and security. Basically, not using deprecated or weak encryption protocols, such as WEP, on public networks. And these can include 802.11, Bluetooth, GSM, GPS, or satellite.

What's demanded here is that you use some kind of best practice for strong encryption. It can be a NIST one, it can be FIPS, it can be an OWASP one - just use secure protocols. For example, AES or 3DES are examples of strong encryption. And look, this doesn't just include specific protocols, which are insecure, such as WEP, but also deprecated versions, or older versions of secure protocols, which have vulnerabilities. For example, even SSL or TLS have previous versions that have been cracked, and this is public. This also includes only accepting trusted keys and trusted certificates. Then, 4.2 is about never sending unprotected Personal Account Numbers (PANs) in instant messaging applications. And this includes SMS or email, for example.

So, employees should not send Personal Account Numbers (PANs) at all in these mediums, if they can - or if they do so, they need to make sure they're encrypted. Or masked, for example. It's very similar to that sub-requirement of Requirement #3. Not showing them in plaintext. But in Requirement #3, we were talking about not STORING them, in Excel or email in plaintext. This is the counterpart. Don't SEND them, in transit, in plaintext. So, make sure to encrypt them, or mask them, or tokenize them, or hash them - if possible, more than one! The logic here is the same - make sure that, if an attacker intercepts your email, or SMSs from employees, they get nothing! And also, there should be a policy defining this. People should not just do this ad hoc.

There must be a process for it. For example, "Every time that you send an email that contains a full Personal Account Number, make sure to encrypt it with AES256". Done. As a good segue to the previous point, sub-requirement 4.3 is our usual one. "Document and enforce all of these policies and procedures". So, encryption procedures, prohibition of sending PANs in plaintext... should be known and enforced by all employees of the organization that deal with Cardholder Data transmission. What are some examples? The first is that not sending this data is OK. Look, if your company can get by without employees sending the Personal Account Numbers through instant messaging or email, that's the best choice! It avoids encryption needs altogether.

Remember, the best way to protect data, is to not even have it in the first place. An example is: You have a customer service representative, that's escalating a case internally. Instead of saying, "We have a problem with order 556, and this credit card number", they can just say, "We have a problem with order 556", and the other person has a way to obtain the credit card number from that order, from some internal system. You transmitted the credit card number without actually having to transmit it! Another example is the FIPS standard. And FIPS stands for "Federal Information Processing Standards". It's the set of encryption standards used by many US institutions - including military and intelligence ones. It includes AES, both 128 and 256 encryption, 3DES, and others.

And, finally, policy enforcement is especially important in this requirement. It's important in all of them, naturally. But in this one, it's especially important, because this is counterintuitive. Let me explain. If you tell people that they need to change management for firewall rules, they were expecting that, to some degree. Or to not turn off their antivirus. But setting a procedure for how credit card data is sent in emails, or instant messages is less natural. So, employees tend to resist it more. That's why you need a policy. Remember, ONE employee sending a full Personal Account Number (PAN) in plaintext in ONE email immediately makes you fail compliance.

What are the key takeaways for this chapter? The first is that this requirement is all about protecting the public. It's about protecting Cardholder Data when they're transmitted across public networks. It's about using strong encryptions, and strong practices of protection when communicating these data. 3.1 is very simple. Use strong encryption, that's it. Use strong encryption protocols, such as WPA, or WPA2, and best practices, such as only new versions of those protocols, only trusted keys, or only trusted certificates. Then, 3.2 is about not sending plaintext Personal Account Numbers (PANs) in instant messages - including email.

Very straightforward. If you are going to send full card numbers, at least mask them, or encrypt them. That's it. And, finally, 3.3 is our customary sub-requirement about documenting and enforcing. So, all of these previous points must not be done informally, but with formal procedures that employees know and put to use. So, as we see, this requirement is mostly about protecting data when transmitted. Best practices, such as strong encryption, the latest version of encryption protocols, never sending data in cleartext, and more.

Requirement 5: Prevent Malware

Let's take a look at Requirement #5, with the simplified name of "Prevent Malware". It's about having antivirus, but similar to the firewall, it's not only about having it, but using it, and treating it in a sophisticated manner. So let's take a look. Requirement #5, with the full name of "Protect all systems against malware and regularly update antivirus software or programs", is very simple: It's about keeping an antivirus software to prevent malware on machines that deal with Cardholder Data (CHD) in specific, therefore, eliminating vulnerabilities. It's also pretty straightforward in terms of sub-requirements.

The first is to actually have antivirus software on commonly affected systems. The second is to frequently update the software, frequently run scans, and frequently save the logs from those scans. In other words - you don't just need antivirus software, you need to actually run it! The third requirement is that antivirus software not be disabled by individual users. One vulnerable computer is all that's enough to let an attacker in. So, there should be a policy preventing users from disabling their antivirus. And, finally, sub-requirement 5.4 is the usual "document and enforce" requirement. All of these procedures must be put on paper, and put to use by personnel.

So, let's start with 5.1. You need to have antivirus software on commonly affected systems. Now, here's the key. The definition of "commonly affected" can vary. These are systems that are regularly accessed, or that regularly connect to networks. And that, naturally, deals with Cardholder Data (CHD). But, depending on how you interpret it, you can include more or less machines. And note that this is irrelevant of the operating system version or type. Naturally, Windows servers are more vulnerable. But don't fool yourself. Mac and Linux also are vulnerable - even if a lot less. So, you always need antivirus.

Again, the definition of what's "commonly accessed" is not a specific one. Just use common sense. For example, if you have an isolated machine, in a locked server room, that's not commonly accessed. But what about a machine that connects to the Internet, even with a firewall, once a month? Or once per quarter? It can be considered or not. Look, the requirement here is not very strict. As with many other criteria, just have a reason for what you selected. It's important that a review of what is "commonly accessed" be frequently done. This is for the same reason as many other requirements. As time goes by, vulnerabilities change, technology changes, and your own devices change.

So, a machine that is "commonly accessed" today may not be three months from now. Or vice-versa. Then, sub-requirement 5.2 is about frequent updating, scanning, and logging. In other words, it's about forcing you to actually put the antivirus to use. Periodic scanning of the machines and retention of these logs is required. The lack of antivirus scanning is only acceptable with a strong reason. For example, maybe you have a server that's so old, or overloaded, that it can't run antivirus - or it would not be able to do anything else! - and maybe, to compensate, you run antivirus software on all machines that connect to it. Again, these kinds of exceptions are acceptable, as long as you have a reason.

Use common sense. Please notice that log retention is also important. And while this may be easy for smaller organizations, it can become a problem for bigger, distributed ones. These logs must be coordinated in some way. Usually, the antivirus logging policy of the software itself will coordinate this, and you can change it. But it must be there. It's not acceptable to have 50 machines connected to one database, each with their own antivirus logs, and if the assessor asks you, "Where are these centralized?", you say, "I don't know". They must be coordinated in some way. Sub-requirement 5.3 is about the antivirus program not being disabled by individual users.

So, people cannot just turn off the antivirus because it slows down the machine, or because they don't like it - even worse, for example, if someone is trying to read a pirated movie on their work computer, and they turn off the antivirus, because it's messing with the torrent program, OK. So, no turning off the antivirus. And this should be an ironclad rule. And yes, you've guessed it: This should not be done informally, but formally through user policy controls. The machine users don't have permissions to turn off the antivirus due to their role. Period. Now, this being said, there can be exceptions for short periods of time.

But these must have a very strong reason - and must be approved by management. For example, the user may go into a locked room, disconnected from any network, and run a CPU-intensive program. For example, to process large batches of data. For one hour. And then, turns the antivirus back on, and runs a scan immediately after. That's acceptable. But, again, it should have a strong reason. And then, we have our old friend. Document and enforce these policies and procedures. Everything we mentioned - from user roles that can't disable the antivirus, to the installation procedure for new machines, to automatic updates, and automated scans - must be documented and known by employees.

And, Of course, put to use. What are some examples here? The first is the definition of "commonly affected". This is another example of an area where PCI-DSS are relaxed. And this is just the minimum requirement. For example, air-gapped machines, or mainframes are not included. But they could be under different information security standards. Then, remember. Strong reasons. Individual users can request to turn off their antivirus temporarily, but they need a good reason to do it. For example, as mentioned, a CPU-intensive operation, isolated from the network. And, finally, "frequent" here is key. Antivirus software must be "frequently" updated, "frequently" run scans, and "frequently" log results. But what's "frequent"? Again, there's not a specific definition, but it has to be something that makes sense. It can be once a week, or even once in two weeks.

But, for example, once every two months is not common sense. It's dangerous. What are our key takeaways for Requirement #5? First, the gist of it is to prevent malware. Constantly running antivirus software, on all machines, that is regularly updated, regularly runs scans, regularly logs the results, and that cannot be turned off. 5.1 defines that you must have antivirus software on all commonly affected machines. No exceptions. Even if the host operating system seems safe. Then, 5.2 is about frequently updating, scanning, and logging. In other words, it's putting the antivirus to use. Keeping it updated - because of new vulnerabilities - frequently scanning - in case you got infected in the meantime - and regularly logging - because you need proof of those scans, as well as what may be in there.

Then, 5.3 is about users not being able to individually turn off the antivirus in their machines if they just feel like it. There can be specific exceptions, with good justifications. But, otherwise, they cannot remove the antivirus. And, finally, sub-requirement 5.4 is our old friend. Document and enforce all policies and procedures that we mentioned. The installation of antivirus on computers, user access controls to not let them remove the antivirus, and so on. They must be on paper, and they must be put to use. So, as we see, Requirement #5 can be simplified as having an antivirus solution, but also, using it in an effective manner. Access control, updates, regular scans, and much more.

Requirement 6: Develop Securely

Let's talk about Requirement #6, with the simplified name of "Develop Securely". It is about including security requirements in your development practices, but it's more than that. It's about training, it's about evaluating changes to the code, and much more. Let's take a look. Requirement #6, with the full name of "Develop and maintain secure systems and applications" is about securing both your own developed applications and software that's off the shelf. With the focus being mostly on your own software. It's important to note that this is one of the most elusive requirements, for one simple reason: That is, in your own software development life cycle (SLDC), developers usually care about functionality, and not security.

Look, they usually want to create interfaces, structure highly efficient database queries, create lightning-fast caching mechanisms, but they're usually not very excited to check for security features. Encrypting communications, avoiding cross-site scripting, buffer overflows, and so on. In fact, many development teams don't even know about these - or they do, but they don't care. This requirement forces you, as we'll see, to put security features into practice. We have 7 sub-requirements this time. First, it's about doing regular vulnerability assessing and risk ranking - both for your applications and off-the-shelf ones. And the reason is sub-requirement 6.2, which is about timely patch installation. Once you rank the vulnerabilities, you want to install patches for the critical ones as soon as possible.

And, as we'll see, there's a different timing for critical patches and all other ones. Then, 6.3 is about having a secure software development life cycle (SDLC). In short, you have to include security requirements in the software development process. And make sure that developers actually implement them. Then, 6.4 is about development change controls. In other words, analyzing the consequences of a new version of developed software, and re-running security tests if there are significant changes. As well as allowing for rollbacks, in case something goes wrong. 6.5 is about secure development training. The only way to make sure that common exploits are avoided is if your development team is trained on how to protect against them.

Then, 6.6 is about preventing public vulnerabilities. It only applies if you have public-facing applications. You simply need to keep track of the vulnerabilities in those public-facing applications more frequently. Because, since they're public, they're more easily targeted. And 6.7 is our usual "document and enforce all policies and procedures" requirement. So all of this must be put on paper, and put to use. The first sub-requirement is 6.1. Vulnerability and risk ranking. What this means is that, every time a third-party vendor publishes a vulnerability, you want to rank it for your specific environment.

And notice, vulnerability information doesn't just come from the manufacturers themselves! It may come from information security communities - maybe someone cracked a protocol, or an application - it may come from publications, or others. The goal is that this identification and risk ranking is what would result in classifying a patch as "critical", or not, depending on the risk of that vulnerability. Because critical patches must be installed within 30 days. And that's a good segue to 6.2, which is about timely patch installation. It's the follow-up to the previous sub-requirement. You want to install patches soon. And here's the key: There's a specific timeline for patches. Critical patches must be as soon as possible - so, within 30 days.

Period. Other lower-risk patches must be within 2 to 3 months. You need to assume that, after this time period, when a vulnerability is published, the whole world knows about it. And attackers are actively scanning for applications and systems that they can exploit. So, installing timely patches is not an option. If you fail to install even one critical patch, within 30 days, you will fail PCI-DSS compliance. And notice that these patches apply to all software in the CDE. So, I'm talking about payment applications, Cardholder Data (CHD) transfer applications, cardholder storage servers, and everything else. Sub-requirement 6.3 is about having a secure software development lifecycle (SDLC). It's the elusive part of this requirement.

It's getting your developers to care about security! So, your own development lifecycle must include security requirements. In short, let's say that you are a bank, rolling out a new payment application. Where are the security requirements? For example, all traffic protected by TLS, or SSL, avoiding cross-site scripting, and more. Are there even security requirements? You would be shocked at the number of organizations that develop payment applications - and big name ones - and literally have no security requirements in their requirement list. Zero. And, by the way, this is regardless of methodology. Whether it's waterfall, or agile, or any other. And it's regardless of the application as well.

Whether it's an application to send money to friends, to pay for products, or to manage your personal credit cards, it doesn't matter. You need the same security requirements. Many organizations think that some applications that are more formal, such as a payment application need more security than an informal one, for example, to transfer money to friends, but in terms of IT, they both store or transmit Cardholder Data (CHD), and they're both vulnerable to attack. Period. And also be aware that this can fail at all stages of the process. So it may be the case that I mentioned - where you don't even have security requirements - or they can be raised, but not actually developed. They're pushed down the priority list. Or they can be developed, but not tested.

Or they can fail at any other point. Consider the following: if the security requirements don't end up working in the production version, you failed. That's it. It's that simple. So, training developers on secure code - which will come later - is a key part of this. They must be aware of all possible attacks, and prevent that while coding. And, finally, code reviews of developed code before deployment by peers are required. Sub-requirement 6.4 is about change controls in developed applications. It has the goal of preventing security vulnerabilities, in case you make a change, for example, that breaks a security feature. So, first the environments must be separated - if they're not already. This shouldn't even be PCI-DSS-required, it's just good development practices! Development and Testing must be separate environments from Production.

Period. And possibly, even separate themselves. Then, Development or Testing credentials and accounts must be removed in Production. And I'm talking about fake users, fake data, or everything else. And this is a good practice, because, sometimes, developers use real data from the database for development, but then, they don't take that data out in production, and you end up with an application that has a small batch of real credit card numbers. As you're guessing, that's not very secure. Then, it's important to retest the application for PCI-DSS compliance after significant changes. And I mean both significant security changes or just significant feature changes.

So, for example, if you have a banking application, and you did risk assessment, and vulnerability assessment, and you roll out a new set of features around peer-to-peer payment that it didn't have before, that app needs to be retested. Now, again, the definition of "significant changes" is subjective. But use common sense. If you completely change your application, and you don't retest it, you will fail compliance! Then, 6.5 is about secure development training. In short, the only way to address common vulnerabilities in development, to minimize exploits, is to train developers to protect against them. And, notice that I don't mean ANY of these, I mean ALL of these.

There is a full list on the PCI-DSS reference manual, but examples include: First, code injection. SQL injection, operating system command injection, such as in Linux. Also, buffer overflows. Then, insecure encryption or key management. I'm both talking about weak encryption protocols, or weak key management. For example, including the encryption keys in the source code of the program. Another: insecure communications, protocols, or ports, that allow an attacker to exploit these vulnerabilities. Also, improper error handling. For example, telling an end user more than what they should know in the logging entries, including local addresses, database credentials, and others.

Remember, it's not just the developers who read the logs! Or cross-site scripting (XSS), or access control vulnerabilities. All of these must be accounted for in the development of all applications within the Card Data Environment (CDE). Then, 6.6 is only applicable if you have public-facing applications. And this is about preventing public vulnerabilities. In other words, because your apps face the public, they are a lot more exposed to attack. So they must be reviewed especially frequently. The reviews can either be done through manual, periodic, reviewing by a specialist, or with an automated tool. Again, common sense. As long as they're tested, that's fine. The imposed periods by the PCI-DSS are at least once per year, but also on every significant change.

So, same example as previously: if you have a banking application facing the public, even if a year has not passed, if you develop a set of new features, and they're very significant, you have to test for public vulnerabilities again. Because it's a significant change. The logic here is that new vulnerabilities are going to show up at least once a year - and they're definitely going to show up if you roll out new features!

Then, 6.7 is our old friend. Document and enforce these policies and procedures. And make sure that the employees - in this case, in specific, the developers - are aware of the policies and procedures.

They have to develop securely, other employees need to identify vulnerabilities, install patches, and so on. Whoever is the owner of these tasks must make them happen. What are some examples? The first are common vulnerabilities. These can almost be considered a checklist in terms of development and testing. They're very known, and they've been here for a long time. Check for injections. Check for buffer overflows. Check for cross-site scripting. And all others. You can literally create a checklist for your developers. They're all known, and they're all easy to protect against. They just have to do it! Then, remember the patching timeline varies.

While the timeline for installation of critical patches is not negotiable, for other patches it is. It does need to make sense, however, as in many other requirements. So, if other patches are installed within 2 months, because that's synchronized with the regular vulnerability testing practice, that makes sense. But if they're installed after two months "just because", then you fail this requirement! Then, remember that failure to address security requirements can occur at any point of the software development life cycle (SDLC). For example, password requirements. Maybe they're never raised in the first place. Maybe they're raised but they're not developed.

Maybe they're developed, but they're not tested. Or any other variation. Remember, if they're not rolled out to production, fully functional, you fail this requirement. What are the key takeaways for this requirement? The first is that it's about developing securely. Securing both third-party applications, but also your developed ones. In the case of your own developed ones, you want to develop them securely, and in the case of both types, you want to isolate them from vulnerabilities, and patch those vulnerabilities. Then, 6.1 is about risk ranking. Analyzing vulnerabilities from third parties, and ranking the criticality of the vulnerabilities. And, then, 6.2 is just installing the appropriate patches for those vulnerabilities.

Critical ones within a month. All other ones between 2 to 3 months. Then, 6.3 and 6.4. 6.3 is about including security requirements in your development lifecycle, while 6.4 is about controls on versions that were already pushed. They must be tested for security vulnerabilities, and include rollback options. So, this is BEFORE the development, and this is AFTER the development. 6.5 is about training developers to care about security vulnerabilities. Injections, buffer overflows, and all others. 6.6 is a specific sub-requirement for public-facing applications. If your application is public-facing, it must be tested more frequently. Period. Once per year, or on any significant change. And, finally, 6.7 is our "document and enforce" sub-requirement.

All of these that we talked about should not be done informally. Everything should be on paper, and put to use by employees. Risk assessment, vulnerability assessment, developer training, patching timelines, testing and rollback for pushed versions... all of these on paper and put to use. So, as we see, Requirement #6 is about developing securely. It is about making sure that the security requirements are developed, and that they end up in production applications, but it's about the whole environment around it. The training, checking for risks, gauging the impact of changes, and a lot more.

Requirement 7: Need-to-Know Access

Let's talk about Requirement #7, with the simplified name of "Need-to-Know Access". And this requirement is nothing more than the embodiment of a security principle called the PoLP - or the Principle of Least Privilege. In other words, every person must have the least information possible in order to do their job, and have the least permissions possible to do their work. Let's take a look. Requirement #7, with the formal name of "Restrict access to Cardholder Data by business need to know" is all about restricting access by employees based on their roles. It follows the PoLP - or the Principle of Least Privilege. In other words, everyone must have the minimum permissions possible to perform whatever it is that they're doing. If the person must only see the full Personal Account Number (PAN), and nothing else, allow them to just see that.

If they can only see a masked Personal Account Number, then allow only that. If they can do their whole job without even looking at card data, even better! It truly is a need-to-know policy. No information is shown by design. All of it is by pure necessity! We have 3 straightforward sub-requirements for this one: The first is limiting Cardholder Data and systems to the required individuals. Self-explanatory. The second is having an established formal Access Control mechanism to formalize this. And then, our usual requirement of documenting and enforcing all these policies and procedures. Sub-requirement 7.1 is limiting Cardholder Data and systems to the required individuals - and the name says it all, really.

As we mentioned, if any person can have less access, do it. If they don't need access at all, then remove it altogether. The less people that have access to sensitive data, the less danger of leaks and attacks that you have. There are less weak points. This is usually established with formal roles. Every personnel role must have specific access privileges, and these privileges must be the minimum possible. For example, maybe there is a role of database administrator that deals with the purging of card data, by comparing the last usage data against the usage of a web platform. Do they even need to see the whole card data, in this case? Probably not.

They can probably see a masked version, and match the two without needing to see the full PAN. Or they can even access these data through a web interface, that's internal, versus accessing the database themselves. This will be more than enough to know which numbers are OK to delete. That's what we're talking about. And naturally, they just need to have delete permissions to purge the data - and possibly, read permissions, naturally - but they don't need edit permissions, for example. You see my point. We're going very deep in terms of what they need to see, and what they can do with it. There are many mechanisms that can achieve this, from Active Directory, to LDAP protocols, Access Control Lists (ACLs), or more. Again, common sense.

It doesn't matter what you use, as long as you achieve the goal. Then, sub-requirement 7.2 is about established access control. It's precisely about this type of system. That is, there must be a system that allows privileges based on the user's role, and that, in case of default, denies all access. Usually, these roles are mapped to the person's job title, such as POS operator, data analyst, database administrator, and many other types that may interact with card data. One very important thing to notice is that these systems must cover roles and privileges for ALL system components in the Card Data Environment (CDE). All firewalls, routers, databases, servers, apps, everything! Nothing can be left out of this. And, finally, sub-requirement 7.3 is our usual known one.

All of these procedures and policies must be documented and enforced. They must be documented on paper - or not literally on paper, but you know what I mean - and they must be enforced by all employees that deal with Cardholder Data (CHD). What are some examples? The first is the philosophy of reducing, reducing, reducing. There are many situations where employees are not required to have access to different components of Cardholder Data (CHD), or different systems. And attention to detail is key here. Go deep into their operations, and see where it is that you can decrease access - or even remove it. Every reduction that you make is another attack vector that's mitigated. Then, use common sense for systems.

The choice of which system to use for access control - from Active Directory, to LDAP - is subjective, as long as it gets the job done, and actually enforces access control. It doesn't matter how you achieve the goal, just achieve it! And finally, changes in access control - as in many other systems - should be change-managed. They should not be done unofficially, but through a formal change management process. So John can't just say to the Active Directory admin, "Hey, man, besides reading card data, my team would like to be able to delete it as well", and the admin says, "OK, done". That should not happen, OK? Formal change management! What are our key takeaways? The first is that this requirement is about having the least possible privilege. Only what the person needs to know.

And then, having systems in place to make that institutionalized. The first sub-requirement is about limiting access. Access to data and to systems by users must be the minimum possible, defined by the roll. The next sub-requirement is about Access Control. There must be a system in place that determines these permissions, based on the person's role, or job description - and remember, that covers all users, all data, and all systems. And finally, 7.3 is our usual "document and enforce" requirement. All policies and procedures must be documented. And they must also be enforced by all employees that deal with these systems, and with Cardholder Data (CHD). So, as we see, this requirement is about giving people access to the least information possible, and giving them the least permissions possible to isolate vulnerabilities, in case of compromise. And not just doing this, but reflecting it on access control, on documentation, and policies.

Requirement 8: Identify Access

Let's talk about Requirement #8, with the simplified name of "Identify Access". This requirement is about the principle of non-repudiation. That is, every action that is taken has a user associated with it, and it can't be ambiguous. You can identify exactly who took what action. Let's take a look. Requirement #8, with the formal name of "Identify and authenticate access to system components", is, in short, about identification. It's about making sure that whoever authenticates for operations is really who they say they are. This is important for one single reason: accountability. In case that an attack happens, you want to know which specific action was taken, or who was compromised. We do have a couple of sub-requirements here, but they're all relatively straightforward.

The first is implementing identification management procedures. So, unique IDs, automatic lockouts, automatic logouts, and so on. Then, strong authentication for all users. Passwords with strict standards and identifying users before any major changes to credentials. The third sub-requirement is Multi-Factor Authentication (MFA) access to the card environment. It can be a combination of password and SMS, password and a physical device, or other combinations. 8.4 is our usual "document and enforce policies and procedures", but specifically, for these 3. This requirement is almost split into halves, and this one is the first one. Then, 8.5 is about avoiding group, shared, or generic IDs.

The "admin" user, the "guest" user... to make sure every action is taken by an identifiable user. After that comes 8.6. Individual physical security measures. What this means is that, whether you use an identity badge, or a fob, or whatever it is, nobody else in the organization can use it as well. Only you. 8.7 is about restricting the actual database access only to database admins. In short, everybody else that wants to access card data will access it through an interface, or whatever it is. But they don't get access to the actual database. And finally, we have the "document and enforce" sub-requirement for this group of procedures and policies. So, let's dive in. 8.1 is about implementing identification management procedures. In short, making sure that every user is identifiable.

First, this means everyone has a unique ID. Period. And it must be properly managed. So access must be revoked for deleted users, as well as revoking accounts that have been inactive for 90 days. Then, access by third parties, such as service providers, or contractors, must be very well-managed, with time limits. Every supplier or contractor that logs in must have very specific permissions that expire after a very specific timeframe. Another point is setting automatic lockouts for failed login attempts. The minimum here is a lockout of 30 minutes for every 6 failed logins. And, finally, automatically logging out users after 15 minutes of inactivity, to prevent attackers from taking advantage of unattended terminals. That's sub requirement 8.1. Then, 8.2 is about strong authentication.

So, users have to authenticate with a measure that is considered "strong" - that's very tied to their own identity. So, strong passwords, real-world objects, such as fobs, or badges, or even biometrics. Things that really tie the action to the person. Passwords should be encrypted when transmitted, as well as stored. It doesn't matter how strong passwords are, if you are storing them in plaintext, if an attacker gets in, they'll have access to everything! Also, there must be a verification of a user's identity before any credential change. So, if John suddenly asks to change their password, or their permissions, the admin must request them to use a strong authentication measure, before doing it. Naturally, this is to prevent an attacker from changing someone's account details. Then, we have minimum password requirements, as well as frequent password changes. At least once every 90 days.

Then, every new password must be different from the last 4 used - or, in other words, if you change them once every 90 days, then you can't use any password that you've used in the last year. And passwords must also be reset on the first use of the account, and the first change of details of that account. Sub-requirement 8.3 requires that any access to the Card Data Environment (CDE) systems or data requires Multi Factor Authentication (MFA). And notice that it's not 2-factor, it's multi-factor. So you have to use at least 2 methods - but you can use more. We mentioned 3 possible methods in the previous chapter: Password, some kind of real-world object, or biometrics, such as a fingerprint. Multifactor requires at least 2 of these.

So it may be a password and identity badge, it may be an identity badge and fingerprint, fingerprint and password, or all three! So, notice, Multifactor Authentication is required on all non-console admin access. And in the case of all users they are performing remote network access, as well. Which has, naturally, increased exponentially since COVID-19. So, if you are an administrator performing any access that's not directly in a console, you need Multi Factor Authentication. And, if you're any person connecting remotely, you need it as well. Then, sub-requirement 8.4 is our usual "document and enforce" for these procedures.

So, it's making sure that practices for password changes, Multi Factor Authentication, and others are properly documented and enforced by employees. Then comes 8.5. This sub-requirement demands that no group IDs, no shared IDs or no generic IDs be used. It's the complement to having unique IDs. So people must use IDs that clearly identify them, and they can't use any ID that doesn't clearly identify them. It may sound a little bit redundant, but it's important to clarify. So this means disabling or removing public user IDs. It also means not allowing any shared ID for any admin function. So nobody can do anything with the "admin" account, or "root" account, but you can and must create individual admin accounts for every person.

It's important to clarify that system or service accounts can exist, but they can't be used by humans. What I mean is that, you can have an "admin" account or "root" account that logs in and performs routine tasks. You just can't have any personnel use those accounts. So these accounts can exist - they just cannot be used by employees. Additionally, it's important to note that, if the organization is a service provider, they should use unique IDs for each of their customers as well. This is almost the reverse of the previous points. So all users that access your environment must be unique. And you, yourself, must have a unique ID for every client environment that you provide a service to. In other words, it's so that if YOU cause a vulnerability, the client can track it back to you, and you can also track it to the specific account for that specific client.

Then, sub-requirement 8.6 is about using individual physical security measures. What I mean is that, whatever physical measure you use, from smart cards, to fobs, identity badges, and others, they cannot be shared among people. They must be used by one user only each. So there must be mechanisms in place - either physical or logical - to make sure that other accounts cannot use this device. An automated one is using Multi Factor Authentication (MFA) for them. For example, you swipe an identity badge to enter a room, but you must input the user's password as well. Or they can be physical. For example, having a member of security identify every person that walks into a room. Naturally, some of these are less costly than others.

But the goal is to make sure that other accounts cannot use this device or object. So, if John has an identity badge, and there's a physical vulnerability, you want to make sure that John was the only person that could have swiped that badge. Sub-requirement 8.7 is very simple. It demands that database access to the Card Data Environment (CDE) is performed not by any user, except database administrators. And even these will have strict security measures. What I mean is that, let's say that you're a credit analyst, at a bank. And you want to take some account numbers to match them with loans. You are not a database administrator. You should NOT be able to run a query on the database.

You will have some sort of internal application that can display those card numbers, but you should never have access to the database itself. So, only database admins (DBAs) with access can run direct queries. And here's something interesting: even applications should have limits on them. So, if any application accesses the database, there must be a specific ID for it. There can't be a shared ID. So if you have a mobile app API, and a web app API, that both run database queries, each one of these must have a unique database user that runs those queries. And only those queries. They can't use a generic user. And, finally, our old friend returns. 8.8 is about documenting and enforcing all policies and procedures.

So, no shared IDs, unique physical access measures, strong authentication, and so on, must all be documented and all enforced by employees. Remember, they cannot be done informally. What are some examples? The first is the 90-day inactivity period. It's important to notice here that there may be exceptions. For example, there may be legitimate reasons for why people may be inactive for 90 days. Vacation, parenthood leave... I guess more parenthood leave, than vacation, for 3 months! But anyway, there may be legitimate reasons for the inactivity. In a good IT system, the user management system is aware of the exceptions. It has some kind of connection to the HR status, to make sure that someone doesn't get back from their parenthood leave, and they find out that their account is gone.

Then, one of the areas where the PCI-DSS are not very demanding is password requirements. You can take a look at the full ones in the reference guide, but although these password requirements are strict, there are other standards that are much more strict! And, finally, there's a reason why it's Multifactor and not 2-Factor Authentication, and the reason is that the PCI-DSS only demands 2, but you can go beyond them. If you really want to protect your organization, you can demand password, SMS, and fingerprint scan for an operation. Maybe even more! So, what are our key takeaways for Requirement #8? The first is that this requirement is all about identifying users.

When an attack occurs, you want to be able to trace it to the source. And I mean both logically and physically! And both in terms of a specific user, and a specific app or system. Sub-requirement 8.1 dictates that user IDs must be unique, and have automatic lockouts, and automatic logouts, while sub-requirement 8.2 mandates strong password practices and encryption, such as regularly changing the password after certain periods of time, or at key events. 8.3 dictates Multifactor Authentication (MFA) for all types of admin access, and remote access. While 8.4 is the usual "document and enforce" for all of these procedures so far. Then, we have sub-requirement 8.5. No shared IDs, or public IDs. Only individual ones.

While sub-requirement 8.6 dictates that there must be unique physical access measures - not used by more than one unique user, under any circumstance. Then, 8.7 dictates that the database should never be directly accessed by anyone except administrators. And even applications, or systems running queries, must have unique users. Then, our last sub-requirement is the usual "document and enforce" for these sub-requirements. Making sure that these database restrictions, shared user ID restrictions, and physical authentication conditions are documented and put to use by employees.

So, as we see, this requirement focuses on a lot of measures. Logical security - such as strong passwords - physical security - such as smart cards, or other physical measures only used by logged users - but, at the end of the day, we want to make sure that if a certain user performs an action, we really know that it was that person, and it can't be anybody else using their account. So there is non-repudiation: For every action, there is a user associated, without any type of ambiguity.

Requirement 9: Restrict Physical Access

Let's talk about Requirement #9, with the simplified name of "Restrict Physical Access". This requirement is all about physical controls. Controlling visitors, physical media, and a lot more. It's about all the ways to physically protect media with data. Let's take a look. Requirement #9, with the full name of, "Restrict physical access to Cardholder Data (CHD)", is about protecting premises, people, and physical media that are in contact with Cardholder Data (CHD). It's the physical equivalent of Requirement #7. We do have a considerable list of sub-requirements this time, but they're all very simple and specific. 9.1 is about entry controls. Cameras or badge authentication, for doors, for specific rooms.

9.2 is about making sure that visitors are distinguished from personnel. It can be as simple as having IDs with a different color, and they must have their access limited. 9.3 is about restricting physical access - that is, access control of specific locations where Cardholder Data is processed or stored, that contain servers, or hard drives, or other physical media where they are. 9.4 is about authorizing visitors. So, visitors must be accompanied and they must have badges that clearly identify them. Also, you must have visitor logs, and you must request expired badges from leaving visitors. 9.5 is about storing media securely.

Being in locked rooms with access control, for example, with biometric unlocking - and this goes both for actual media, such as hard disks and USB drives - but also printed paper records with Cardholder Data (CHD). 9.6 is not about storing, but it's about distributing media securely. It's about having processes to transport media that contains card data, such as hard drives, or USB drives, including tracking it when sent by mail, and having management awareness - or approval. for transporting it. 9.7 is about strict media storage and accessibility.

So, having an inventory of all physical media with Cardholder Data, to immediately be aware of something that may be wrong with them, or if any of them go missing.

9.8 is about securely destroying not-needed media. Whatever media contains Cardholder Data (CHD), whether paper, or a hard drive, it must be destroyed securely. It doesn't matter if it's shredding, burning, or demagnetizing, but there must be a destruction certificate. 9.9 is about protecting devices, in specific, that capture card data, such as POS systems at a coffee shop. They should not be tampered with, and personnel must be trained to detect if they ARE tampered with. And, finally, 9.10 is our usual "document and enforce" requirement for all of these policies and procedures. Let's start with 9.1: Enforcing entry controls. Very straightforward. This is about controlling the entry of users with access to Card Data Environment (CDE) systems and data.

So, one of two choices: you must either have cameras OR access control, such as locked doors unlocked with biometrics, on all entries and exits, monitored and maintained for 90 days. So, if you have physical media with card data in one room, you need cameras or access control in one room. If you have card data in 20 rooms, you need this for 20 rooms. And you must store the data for 90 days. Note that this also includes securing, for example, device ports, such as USB or network ports, where an attacker could install a keylogger, or another device, as well as restricting access to network access points. It's also important to understand that you need to gather enough user data on people that enter.

So, for example, you don't need just a paper sheet with the date and the name, but you need their role, their permissions, their specific purpose, and more. It has to be more granular. 9.2 is about distinguishing visitors. Very clear. It's about making sure that visitors are easily distinguished from personnel. This is to not allow them to blend in, in case they want to cause some trouble. They're clearly identified. For example, the simple color-coding of badges takes care of this. Personnel have blue badges. Visitors have red ones. Done. But, besides this, note that visitors should also have different access permissions. Naturally.

As well as being properly terminated when they leave. By this I mean, the company must ask for their badge back when they leave. Not doing it is a very subtle - but a very clear - failure of this requirement. You cannot let somebody leave with a credential that gives them access to your premises. Period. 9.3 is about restricting actual physical access. So, sensitive areas where Cardholder Data (CHD) are stored or processed must have restrictive access. So we already stated, in the first sub-requirement, that there must be access control. So, you're aware of who enters. This sub-requirement is about minimizing who enters. So, for any room or environment, who is authorized to come in here? In a, way it's the physical equivalent of Requirement #7.

Remember, that requirement was about minimizing who could access each set of data. And this is about minimizing who accesses each physical set of data. Each room. And, unsurprisingly, it follows the same rationale as Requirement 7. The Principle of Least Privilege (PoLP). Decrease or cut access whenever possible. If this employee doesn't need access to this room, don't allow them in. If they only need to access the room when accompanying another user, with a different role, don't let them come in by themselves! Very simple. Principle #4 is about authorizing visitors. By definition, "visitors" are people who are not familiar with your internal security procedures. That's the definition.

They're not held by the same set of standards as your personnel. So, therefore, they must be controlled! So, first, visitors must be accompanied at all times, in sensitive card data environments, with badges that clearly identify them. These are two faces of the same principle. They must be accompanied, so that they're not alone with Cardholder Data, and they must have clear identification, so that they cannot blend in. This is all to prevent them from possibly attacking you. Also, visitor logs must be capped and expired badges must be surrendered. Again, these are both very important. Not having proper visitor logs, or not demanding a visitor's badge, at the end of the visit, are both enough to fail this requirement. Then, requirement 9.5 is about the physical media themselves.

It's all about storing physical media securely. In other words, any media that contains Cardholder Data (CHD) must be under lock and key. That's it. Subject to strong security measures. And it's important to clarify that "physical media" are not just hard drives, or USB drives, or physical servers - not just electronic systems - but they're also printed versions of Cardholder Data (CHD) in different records. So, even in a very simple environment, such as a coffee shop, for example, where you have paper receipts with Cardholder Data, they must be in a locked room, with strict security measures.

It's also important to annually revisit the security of physical media, for the same reasons as many other requirements. Networks change, people change, vulnerabilities change, the data that you're storing changes, maybe even the card data flow itself might have changed by then. Then, if 9.5 was about storage, then 9.6 is about distribution. If you want your physical media to be secured when stored, then you definitely want them to be secured when distributed. So you need to know what media is distributed, and who it's distributed to. If a hard drive leaves a locked room, and it has a lot of card data, you better know where it went, and who it went to. What you want to do is classify media in terms of data sensitivity, and you want to define which specific roles have access to those media, and why.

For example, you may have a USB stick, with a small backup of card numbers, that are going to be purged, and you may have a master hard drive, with explicit logs, that include Cardholder Data (CHD) of the last 10 years. These two should not have the same sensitivity - and not be handled by the same role! Unless, naturally, there's a strong reason for that. Additionally, moving any media off-site must be approved by management - or at least management must be aware of it - and the transport itself, for example, if it's via mail must be secured and tracked. 9.7 is about strict media storage and accessibility. It's about proper inventorying of the media.

This is crucial, so that you can immediately detect if any media go missing, as well as have a bird's-eye view of the sensitivity of all media contained. And, unsurprisingly, these inventories should be reviewed at least once per year. For the same reasons as usual. Sub-requirement 9.8 is about destroying media that are not needed. Just like we talked about purging unneeded logical data, in Requirement #3, we are now talking about purging physical media that are not needed anymore. And whatever medium they are in - paper, hard drives, USB drives - they should be safely destroyed.

In the case of hard drives, they may be demagnetized, or degaussed, physically destroyed, securely erased (zeroed out), or others, but whatever the medium, proof of completion of the process is necessary. For example, a shredding certificate by the provider, or just a certificate of destruction, in general. In the case of printed materials, these may be shredded, burned, or others, but they require a certificate of destruction as well. Every destruction type requires one. Requirement 9.9 is all about protecting devices that actually capture Cardholder Data (CHD) such as POSs. These are devices that receive payment data, in specific, and they must not be accessible by attackers.

The canonical example is an attacker installing a "skimmer" on your POS, that copies the card numbers. So, there must be an inventory of these, to begin with. Which devices actually capture card data. Then, these devices should be periodically examined for tampering, but more than that, staff should be trained to detect tampering themselves, and to report any suspicious activity, by anyone interacting with the device. Again, using our coffee shop example, the people who are at the register must report if they see anything suspicious. If they think that someone is messing with the POS machine, or placing something on it, they must report it immediately. And they must be able to detect this themselves.

And, finally, 9.10 is our customary requirement about documenting and enforcing all policies and procedures. As with other requirements, everything that we talked about - from visitor distinction, physical restrictions, securely storing media, securely moving it, securely destroying it, and everything else - should be documented. And employees should enforce these policies. What are some examples? POS skimming is the main focus of sub-requirement 9.9. We are trying to prevent the practice of skimming - where the attacker installs an additional component, or actually changes the device - for example, on the part of the payment terminal, where you have a card slot, an attacker can install a fake card slot, that couples on top of it, and once installed, the person can't even tell the difference.

It's like a cover, but it captures data in real time - whether the magnetic track or the PIN - and it can do it either locally, or even broadcast it in real time. And staff training is crucial to detect these devices. Then, this requirement is, in many ways, the equivalent of Requirement #7. So, Requirement #7 was about need-to-know access to digital data. This is the physical equivalent. We are minimizing access based on roles and functions. But not access to data, access to physical locations. And, finally, the destruction of both physical and digital media can be done in a myriad ways. But the important thing here is that, at the end of the day, the provider certifies its destruction.

It can be shredded, burned, degaussed, exploded, whatever - but there must be proof that it was done. What are our key takeaways here? First, this requirement is about restricting access. It's all about preventing access, from real-world individuals - both distinguishing them, but also increasing the security of sensitive assets. Then, 9.1 is about enforcing access control physically. Either with cameras or authentication for safe rooms. While 9.2 is about distinguishing visitors. They cannot blend in with other personnel - different badge colors and different access permissions. Then, the next two: 9.3 is about actually restricting access to physical media, and specifically, limiting that access as much as possible, related to the roles of different personnel.

While 9.4 is about authorizing, logging, and accompanying visitors to the premises. Not allowing them to be alone or to have any chance to attack your premises. Then, 9.5 and 9.6 are about physical media. 9.5 is about storing it securely - with physical protection measures - while 9.6 is about moving it securely - with both management awareness, and tracking of the transportation medium. Then, the next two: 9.7 is about inventorying media - cataloging it, so that you immediately know if something is missing, or was compromised. While 9.8 is about securely destroying media. When not needed, it must be disposed of, and with a certificate.

The final two are 9.9 and 9.10. 9.9 is about specifically protecting devices that capture card data. In other words, preventing POS skimming, and similar practices. Both in terms of protecting the devices, from attackers, but training your own staff to identify the tampering. While sub-requirement 9.10 is about documenting and enforcing these policies and procedures. As usual. All of these points must not be done informally, but they must be documented and enforced by staff. So as we see, this requirement is kind of an umbrella for all types of physical controls to actually protect your data. Dealing with physical media, destroying them, transporting, storing them, physical access to rooms with media, visitor controls, and a lot more.

Requirement 10: Monitor Networks

Let's talk about Requirement #10. It has the simplified name of "Monitor Networks", but it could arguably have an even simpler name, which is "logging". Logging, logging, and more logging. It's about having a system which logs specific types of events, and specific data within those events. But, just like the firewall, or the antivirus, it's not just about having the system, but using it in a sophisticated manner. So let's take a look. Let's talk about Requirement #10. The formal name of this requirement is to "Track and monitor all access to network resources and Cardholder Data". But it might as well be called "logging". Log everything. Keep a constant output of logs, of everything relevant, and protect those logs at all costs.

That's it. It's about logging actions and identifying the root cause of possible attacks. We have 9 sub-requirements this time. The first is to implement audit trails. In other words, have a logging solution. The second is related to the specific types of events that must be logged. All admin events, all intrusions, all operations on card data, and all failed operations. Then, we have specific data that must be logged for each event. Who was the user? What was the operation type? What was the status - whether success or failure? And other elements. Then, 10.4 is about synchronizing all clocks using one mechanism.

This is so that we don't experience inconsistency across different logs of different machines. It's very important to be able to reconcile those logs. 10.5 is to prevent alteration of audit trails. Using a FIM - or File Integrity Monitoring - solution. If a log was tampered with, you will know immediately. 10.6 is about reviewing logs frequently. This is to make possible the discovery of attacks almost instantly. There are specific logs, including for critical components, that must be reviewed daily. 10.7 is very simple. Log retention. Logs must be retained for 1 year total. And out of those 12 months, the last 3 months, in specific, must be immediately available. Then, 10.8 is for service providers.

And it's about detecting and reporting failures timely. It means that, in case the logs indicate that you were compromised - and it could affect your clients - you have to report it immediately, and you have to take care of it immediately. And 10.9 is our old friend. Document and enforce all policies and procedures. So, 10.1 is very simple. Have a logging solution. Everything that is in scope of the Card Data Environment (CDE) must be logged. So, all systems related to Cardholder Data (CHD) must keep some sort of logging activity, and specifically, related to user actions on set systems. So, these logs must cover all systems in the CDE, and they must identify specific users. The second requirement, 10.2, is about logging specific events.

It's about including, in your logging practice, a set of specific events. First, all activity related to accessing Cardholder Data (CHD), or accessing logs themselves. As well as changes in the logging policy itself - changing the frequency, or stopping logs. So, if a user runs a database query on card data, that's logged. If they access the logging system, that's logged. If they change the type of logging done, that's logged. And if they stop the logging system, that must be logged as well. Then, any action taken by administrators or root-privilege users. Whether they create user accounts, change firewall configs - whatever it is. Every action by someone with administrator privileges must be logged.

Then, any type of unsuccessful operation, by any user, at any level. You're probably guessing why: If an attacker, for example, is trying to brute-force a password, there will be multiple failed attempts related to passwords or encryption keys. But this is not just about unsuccessful logins, but any operation, for example, that fails due to not having permissions. For example, an account that tries to change the firewall configuration, but fails, because they don't have permission. That is logged as well. Then, any type of change to user credentials themselves. Or changes in the user accounts themselves. So, if an account is created by a user, that is logged. If you change someone's password, that is logged as well.

As you can see, most of these have to do with actions that an attacker could take, such as unsuccessful attempts to change something, stopping the logging system, doing something with root access, or changing user accounts. If 10.2 told us what types of events to log, then 10.3 tells us, within an event, which specific data to log. In each log entry, specific data points must be included. Namely: First, the user ID of the person. Then, the type of event. Whether it was a failed login, or the logging was stopped, or Cardholder Data (CHD) was viewed, and so on. Then, the date and time of the operation. Then, whether it resulted in success or failure. Also, its origination - that is, the machine where it happened. And finally, the identity of the affected resource.

For example, did I change the firewall configuration for a specific server? Identify that server. Did I run the query on a database? Log which one it is. Did I change a specific datum in the database? Identify which one it is. It's, for example, having a logging entry that says, "David, with user ID 1158, disabled the logging mechanism, with a success code, at 4:31 PM, at server 331 (or with a specific IP address), and the affected logging system was machine 221", for example. This makes sure that all log entries contain useful information to detect attackers. Then, 10.4 is very simple. It's about making sure that all logging mechanisms synchronize their timing through one single mechanism.

This is so we can reconcile different logs, and establish a sequence of events. If you use different machines that have different clocks - or even different time zones - it will be hell to reconcile all logs. So, the goal is to be able to precisely reconcile all logs from different machines. And this helps, especially, to interpret sequential events. You want to know that an attacker gained admin access from a machine at 10:51, and then created another user on another machine, at 10:52. Even one minute of difference prevents you from being able to interpret events sequentially. As usual, it's about common sense.

It doesn't matter what the time source is, but it does matter that this time source is subject to access control - so, not just anybody can come in and change the source - and that any changes to the time synchronization mechanism be logged. Then, 10.5 is about log integrity itself. Due to the importance of logs, they must be maintained. And if you're thinking of File Integrity Monitoring (FIM), you would be completely correct, but it's not just that. It's also backing up logs as soon as possible, so they can't even be tampered with in the first place. Remember, if an attacker tampers with your logs, your whole reporting of events is compromised.

And this sub-requirement includes, for example, first of all, access control to logs by user roles. Just like Cardholder Data (CHD), not just anyone should be able to access the logs. As well as proper backing up of these logs. You want to physically move the files, if they're printed, or move them to different networks - usually, outside the DMZ, so that they are protected from external traffic. Likewise, someone can spy on your credit card receipts logged by the POS, while they're by the counter, where you take payments - if you're a merchant. But, once you move them to a safe room, they are protected. And the idea here is that this should be done promptly.

And the definition of "promptly" is another common sense one. The ideal is as close to real time as possible. But, naturally, this isn't always possible. For example, if your organization is a chain of coffee shops, it's not reasonable that, any time that a POS machine emits a receipt, with credit card data, an employee has to go into the safe room and place the paper there. But they can let the receipts pile up for 15 minutes, or 30 minutes, or every hour, and then move all of them at once. That would still be considered reasonable. But leaving them there for a couple of days is not "promptly". So, again, use common sense. Then, a File Integrity Monitoring (FIM) solution should be implemented to prevent log tampering.

If a log file is altered, you will know right away! After this comes 10.6. Review logs frequently. The goal is to make sure that, if an attack does occur, and it's logged, it's found out ASAP. Ideally, there are automated alerts for this, but manually reading the logs is also essential. For two reasons: Both because some suspicious activities may not trigger alarms - especially, if the attacker knows how to avoid them - or, an advanced attacker may have disabled the log alerts themselves. So, reading logs frequently is crucial. There are specific logs that must be reviewed daily.

For example, logs of all systems that deal with Cardholder Data (CHD), or Sensitive Authentication Data (SAD). Then, all critical components of your Card Data Environment (CDE), and all security attacks - or intrusion attempts. Logs belonging to these categories have to be reviewed daily by someone. Period. Other logs can be reviewed at a periodic pace, which depends on their relative importance. There's not one set rule. Again, just use common sense. Also, it's important to properly review anomalies with a procedure. What I mean is that, if there's a log entry that points to a possible attack, it's not just enough to read it and say "OK". There must be a procedure with follow-up actions.

Almost like a mini-Incident Response (IR) for something suspicious. It's not necessary to take a specific action, you just need to have a plan. Then, 10.7 is about log retention. Very simple. The logs themselves must be retained for 1 year, and out of that last year of data, the last 3 months, in specific, must be readily accessible for review. That's it. This should occur not just in practice, but also be consolidated in formal security or logging retention policies. In other words, it's not just running a crontab process, for example, that's hidden in the server, and that archives all logs after 3 months, and that removes the files after 1 year. It must be an explicit policy...

and then you can run the process! Then, requirement 10.8 is all about detecting and reporting failures immediately. And this is just for service providers. The rationale here is the following: If you're not a service provider, if you're hacked, that's bad. Your information is compromised. But if you ARE a service provider, and you're hacked, that may affect all of your customers as well. So, regular detection and reporting is essential. The type of failures that need to be reported include: Number one, all critical systems, including the Intrusion Detection System (IDS) or Intrusion Prevention System (IPS), any firewall, any File Integrity Monitoring (FIM) solution, any antivirus, any physical or digital access control mechanisms, the logs themselves, and so on.

Any failure in any of these systems means an immediate red flag must be raised. And also, this should be common sense. But it's still spelled out. It can't just be prompt detection - it must be prompt handling. Imagine that you detected something in real time, but you do nothing. You still fail the requirement, OK? You must have a set of processes, and in this case, it literally is a type of Incident Response (IR) to deal with a possible attack. And, finally, our old friend shows up again. Sub-requirement 10.9 is all about documenting and enforcing all of these policies and procedures. In this case, all of the logging retention policies, access control policies, File Integrity Monitoring (FIM), and any procedures that we've spoken about in this requirement must be documented, and must be properly enforced by employees.

What are some examples here? The first is time synchronization. As we mentioned, it's an essential component in the process of interpreting logs of different machines. If logs from different machines have an offset of even 1 minute, or 5 minutes, that's not just confusing - it literally compromises your chances of detecting an attack. Because you can't establish a sequence of events, and, therefore, you can't find the source. Therefore, this is crucial to prevent attacks. Then, proper responses may vary. When we mention, for example, for service providers that you need an Incident Response "plan", that may involve many aspects. Immediately restoring security, documenting the duration of the attack - or possible unavailability of the service - having additional security controls, or others.

You don't need specific steps, you just need to have a plan. And, finally, as with many other requirements, Requirement #10 is correlated with others. In this case, it's correlated with requirements #7 and #8, which are "Need-to-Know Access" and "Identify Access". It's correlated in the sense that, the more that you can control access, by user roles, the more that you can identify specific individuals, and use strong authentication, or Multifactor Authentication (MFA), the more granular the logs will be. You will know exactly where an attack came from, and what accounts were affected. What are our key takeaways here? The first is that this requirement is about logs, logs, logs.

Logging specific events, logging specific data for each event, securing the logs, securing their file integrity, securing their time integrity, retaining them, and reviewing them frequently. The first two sub-requirements are easy. 10.1 is just about having a logging solution. 10.2 is about logging specific events. All administrator actions, all card data changes, all changes to logging itself, and all changes to users. Then, 10.3 is about logging specific data. Identify the user, identify the action, identify the result, and the system affected. 10.4 is about maintaining the same time synchronization for all logging mechanisms. Then, 10.5 is about preventing log tampering. In other words, File Integrity Monitoring (FIM). But also, backing up the actual logs as soon as possible.

Then, 10.6 is about reviewing logs. Reviewing critical ones daily, and the others at a slower pace. Then, 10.7 is about log retention. The last year of logs must be retained, and the last three months, in specific, must be readily available. 10.8 is for service providers. And it's about the timely recognition and response of critical issues. And, finally, 10.9 is our old friend. All of these procedures and policies, throughout the requirement, must be documented, and they must be enforced by employees. So, as we see, just like the firewall, or the antivirus, it's not just about having a logging system, but using it in a sophisticated manner. Log retention, actions on log alerts, and a lot more.

Requirement 11: Test Regularly

Let's talk about Requirement #11, with the simplified name of "Test Regularly", and it's about, well, testing things regularly! Both in the physical world, such as testing for rogue Access Points, and in the logical one, such as vulnerability scanning or penetration testing. Let's take a look. Our second to last requirement, Requirement 11, has the formal name of "Regularly Test Security Systems and Processes". Its main purpose is to have processes and procedures in place to detect and address vulnerabilities of different types. So, if the previous points were about securing data, or systems, or user privileges, this principle is all about actually preventing attacks. Preventing intruders.

Simple and clear. It includes detecting both internal and external threats of multiple types. Remember, attackers may not necessarily come from the outside - they may already be in your system! Some sub-requirements include: First, 11.1 is about detecting Access Points (APs). Both authorized ones and unauthorized ones. And what to do if you find the latter. 11.2 is about internal and external vulnerability scanning. Knowing what you are exposed to. Then, 11.3 takes it one step further and it's about penetration testing. So, if vulnerability scanning is more passive - just knowing what's out there - then, penetration testing is more practical - taking those weaknesses and exploring them in a real-world scenario.

Then, 11.4 is very simple. Have an Intrusion Detection System (IDS) or Intrusion Prevention System (IPS). That's it. Just like a firewall, or an antivirus. Make sure that it's there, and that it's updated. Then, 11.5 is about File Integrity Monitoring (FIM) of files. Making sure that no critical files are tampered with, or changed. And finally, 11.6 is our usual friend! Documenting and enforcing all policies and procedures. Let's start with sub-requirement 11.1. This is about detecting both authorized and unauthorized (or rogue) Access Points (APs) internally. As the name says, you want to run periodic scans to know which Access Points are present internally.

This must be done quarterly. Not only do you need to scan for them, but you must keep an inventory of these - so that you can compare it against the previous version, in each iteration. And here's the thing: depending on the size of your network, this may involve a multitude of tools. Some IDS or IPS systems even perform this kind of scan, or it can also involve actual physical checks of these Access Points, or others. Just make sure that you have a process to find them. You also need Incident Response (IR) procedures, so that, beyond identifying rogue APs, you can actually remedy the situation. Then, sub-requirement 11.2 is about performing both internal and external vulnerability scans. This vulnerability scanning must be done quarterly, as well, but also after significant changes to your systems.

It's important to note that, in this case, they must be performed by what's known as an ASV or Approved Scan Vendor, who are approved by the PCI council themselves. Also, if you're familiar with vulnerability scanning, you will know about the CVSS score - or Common Vulnerability Scoring System score. There's a lot of internal metrics to it, such as temporal and environmental ones, but the gist of it is that your score can be between 0 and 10. Where 0 means you're Fort Knox. No weaknesses! And 10 means you are completely unprotected. And your systems must have a score of 3.9 or lower - which is considered the green area, the "safe" area. On top of it, if there are any specific vulnerabilities which are high-risk, they must be addressed.

Not necessarily right away, but there must be some process to deal with them. Next comes 11.3. This sub-requirement is about penetration testing. It's taking the vulnerability scanning of the previous principle and going even deeper, in practice, on those vulnerabilities. It's important to note that a documented methodology should be used here. No specific one is required - again, use common sense - and usually it will be a methodology that's specific to the company, but there are guidelines for this selection. For example, it must be done at least once a year, and after significant changes. Again, the standards must be documented or industry-accepted.

An example is the NIST SP800-115, but you can select any other acceptable option. Then, it must be extensive. Testing from inside and outside the network, from the app layer, the protocol layer, and so on. And these penetration tests should both review the current threats, but also make recommendations of improvements for the future! It's not just enough to generate an output. There must be recommendations on improvements! Then, compared to the previous two, 11.4 is very simple. Just have an Intrusion Detection or Intrusion Prevention System (IDS/IPS). That's it! It's important to note, though, that this system should cover all critical points within the Card Data Environment (CDE).

All database servers, all key locations, all critical systems - and possibly, other locations that you may find important yourself. It's analogous to the firewall. The firewall must cover all critical network junctures, and the IDS or IPS must cover all critical systems. Additionally, this IDS or IPS system must be kept updated, to detect new attackers. Just like the antivirus or the firewall. Then, 11.5 is about File Integrity Monitoring or change detection. So these systems should cover changes to critical system files, to configuration files, content files, logs, and they should check for changes at least once a week. So, in the logging requirement, we already covered that logs should be under this kind of system.

But now, we're expanding it, and saying that all of these other critical files should be as well. There are some categories that are just natural -

for example, system files. If you're on Windows, the "system32" folder is a must. Or application executable files for all your applications. Or configuration and parameter files, logging audit files, key files, and possibly others, that may be of importance - such as, I don't know, temporary files during operations. And, naturally, there must be a process here to deal with File Integrity Monitoring (FIM) alerts. Some kind of Incident Response procedure. As usual, it's not just enough to know that something went wrong, but something must be done to remediate it. And, finally, 11.6 is our usual sub-requirement.

All of these procedures and policies - about testing techniques, schedules, actions, tools - must be properly documented and enforced by employees. You can't just do them informally. What are some examples of this requirement? The first is vulnerability testing versus penetration testing. These are two terms that are often mistaken, but they are very different, and information security professionals will clearly know this. But, for everyone else, vulnerability testing is passive: It's about reporting on possible vulnerabilities, in general. Penetration testing, however, is super specific. It takes your context and simulates an attack. To use an analogy, if we were talking about you personally, vulnerability testing is you going to the doctor and they say, "Hey, you have a weak heart, you have high tension", whatever it is. These are the weaknesses.

Penetration testing would be an attacker knowing your specific schedule, when you're vulnerable, what you eat and what you drink without noticing, and attacking you with those specific variables. One of them is a scan, while the other is a simulation of an attack with intent to hurt. Then, remember that penetration testing is important both in internal and external terms. I know I've said this, but many companies focus just on protecting the organization from an outside attack. But the key is, what if the attacker is already in? And, finally, defining "critical" is important. As we mentioned, critical files need to be protected by File Integrity Monitoring (FIM). And critical junctions must be defended by IDS or IPS.

And, naturally, there are certain elements that, regardless of interpretation, will always be included - such as databases with card data - but you can expand this definition, if there are other networks or servers that you consider "critical". What are the key takeaways this time? The first is that Requirement 11 is all about testing. It's about securing networks and systems, by making sure to check for vulnerabilities - and simulating external attacks frequently. Requirement 11.1 is about detecting wireless APs. Both legitimate and rogue ones, and having a procedure for what to do with the latter, while 11.2 is about doing vulnerability scanning. At least quarterly, or on significant changes. Requirement 11.3 is about penetration testing. Regularly done.

Both internal and external, and on different layers - while 11.4 is very simple. Have an IDS or IPS system that detects threats in a timely manner. Then, we have two final sub-requirements. 11.5 is about File Integrity Monitoring (FIM) and change detection. In other words, detecting tampering of critical files. While 11.6 is our usual friend. Document and enforce everything. All of these procedures don't just have to be done, they have to be done as a process! So, as we see, Requirement #11 is about testing for vulnerabilities in a periodic manner. We talked about specific systems, such as IDS or IPS systems, pentesting methodologies, and so on, but the general philosophy is to frequently test for different types of vulnerabilities, and to do it with updated tools.

Requirement 12: InfoSec Policy

Up next is Requirement #12, with the simplified name of "Information Security Policy". You can consider this requirement to be the compilation of all the sub-requirements that say, "Document and enforce" on all other requirements, but it's even more than that. It's about screening personnel, assigning owners, and all the bureaucratic parts of information security for cardholder data. If you were expecting the last requirement to take it easy, it's also the biggest one so far! So, let's dive into it. Let's cover the last requirement of the PCI-DSS. Requirement #12 has the full name of "Maintain a policy that addresses information security for all personnel". And, as the name says, it's about having an information security policy at all levels of the organization. This is probably the only requirement in the framework that is not technical, but is about management.

This is fully about policies, as the name says. It's also the requirement where all other policies come together. Do you remember that sub-requirement, at the end of every requirement, saying "document and enforce these policies and procedures"? Well, this is where all of those come together. So, you may see direct references to other requirements here. For example, "Keep an inventory of all physical assets", which comes from Requirement #9. Or, "Keep systems updated", which includes a bit from Requirement #5, keeping the antivirus updated, or Requirement #1, keeping the firewall updated, or Requirement #11, keeping the IDS or IPS updated, and so on. It brings them all together. But it does go beyond it, and it sets even more policies and procedures.

But, anyway, let's cover it. And, by the way, if you were expecting the last requirement to be a little lighter, because we're approaching the end, well, I have bad news for you! This is the most extensive and longest requirement of them all. It covers the whole company, all of the people, and all the processes related to card data. We have 11 sub-requirements this time. So, the PCI-DSS framework really ends with a bang! Anyway, 12.1 is about establishing, publishing, maintaining, and disseminating this policy. It's about making sure that you do have this policy, and that it reaches the people that must know about it. 12.2 is about having an annual risk assessment process. Every year, you must be aware of what threats and what vulnerabilities exist, and plan for them. 12.3 is about developing usage policies.

What technology can be used, by whom, and what are the acceptable uses. 12.4 is about having clear security responsibilities. This one is short. It's just saying, whatever it is - firewall, antivirus, etc - there must be an owner for it. Period. 12.5 is about assigning said responsibilities. It's the flip side of this one.wWhile 12.4 says that there must be an owner, 12.5 says that you have to identify the owner. 12.6 is about security awareness. In other words, your personnel must know how important information security is, from the moment they're hired. Non-negotiable. 12.7 is about screening potential personnel before hiring them. Don't let people into your organization without background checks, reference checks, or others.

12.8 is about your service providers. Third parties that you contract with. You must have a process for their selection, a list of authorized providers, and you must obtain a confirmation, from each, that they will safeguard card data. And if they don't give it to you, something is wrong here.1 2.9 is the direct segue to that point. If you are a service provider, you must provide this confirmation, as safeguarding their card data, to your clients, in writing. 12.10 is about having an Incident Response (IR) plan. In case of a breach, what happens? Not only having it, but testing it every year. Finally, 12.11 is in case you are a service provider. And in that case, just like the security testing, here, you must review your security policies and procedures quarterly. And exactly for the same reasons as the other sub-requirements.

Technology changes, attacks change, and your systems change. Let's start with 12.1. You need to establish, publish, maintain, and disseminate an information security policy. In other words, make the policy reach the people that it impacts, and keep it updated. That's it. The policy must be disseminated to everyone that has roles that deal with Cardholder Data (CHD). In other words, people that are subject to these policies. They must be reviewed yearly. And for the same reasons as for other requirements. The business changes, the technology changes, suppliers change - which results in different types of threats, but also different possible protection techniques. 12.2 is about having an annual risk assessment process. This is, inventorying new threats and vulnerabilities, and repeating this process both yearly, and on significant changes.

And these vulnerabilities must be assessed in terms of risk levels. It's important to note that formal risk analysis results must be an output of this analysis. In other words, something tangible must come from it. Otherwise, you fail the requirement! And also, all critical assets in your Card Data Environment, as well as the threats, and the vulnerabilities, must all be identified. Otherwise, you can't properly assess the risks. In other words, you're asking yourself, "What do I have that's important? And what's weak about it?". That's it. And you repeat this question every year, with a tangible answer. Sub-requirement 12.3 is about developing usage policies. Who uses technological assets, and how.

First, management approval for adopting any type of critical technology. As well as having role-based access control by individual users to that technology. These are mandatory. All assets must be inventoried, as well as all authorized users per asset. And that includes, in specific, the owner of that asset. There must be an owner, not just for any given task, but also any given hard asset. Just to clarify, they don't need to be literally in the next room, but they need to be identified. What I mean is, if one of your firewalls is compromised, who is the owner of it? Because that person will probably be responsible for remedial actions, as well as, in general, keeping it updated and protected. These policies should also define acceptable uses of technology.

For example, can you use a computer that stores cardholder information for sales calls? By a sales representative? Which may represent a lot of unsecured communication calls. And, on a large scale. Or, can people use computers to go on social media, or to read pirated movies? This must be very clear. Also, there must be acceptable network locations and acceptable products. Maybe some protocols are just not accepted, or some vendors are blacklisted - but all of this must be on paper. Then, restrictive remote usage policies for third parties. This stems directly from Requirement #7, "Need-to-Know Access". Third parties must have very specific logins that allow them to do very specific things, and with very specific time durations.

And, then, naturally, prohibiting moving any Cardholder Data (CHD) to local machines. In other words, an employee can't just copy credit card data to their work laptop, to use as mock data - to develop an app, for example - and take it home. Or, if there are exceptions, there must be a very good reason for them. Then, 12.4 is very simple. Have clear security responsibilities for all personnel. So, all responsibilities must be defined. The firewall admin has the responsibility to keep it updated - maybe to update the network documentation as well - maybe there's an office security manager with the responsibility of safeguarding physical data, or verifying visitor badges, and so on.

Every person must have a responsibility. And this goes up the chain, up to the senior managers. There must be someone ultimately responsible for the Information Security policy. Probably a CSO (or Chief Security Officer), or a CISO (or Chief Information Security Officer), or maybe some interchapter with the Data Protection Officer (or DPO). But there must be an owner of some sort. Then, 12.5 is about assigning said security responsibilities. This point includes having ultimately responsible personnel for specific tasks, which can include, for example: First, someone responsible for establishing and disseminating the actual policies. Someone responsible for monitoring all user accounts. As well as all access to Cardholder Data (CHD).

Then, someone responsible for monitoring all security logs, and all alerts. Or someone responsible for establishing Incident Response (IR) procedures and escalation procedures. As well as actually executing them. So, this is a counterpart to the previous point. The previous point said that people must be responsible for something - and this point says that these specific activities must have an owner. They're two sides of the same coin. Then, 12.6 is about having a security awareness program. In the company, making sure that all personnel know the policies and procedures. Both upon recruiting - which is the starting point - but also yearly, due to changes in technology and procedures.

So they have to be trained not just upon hiring, but also yearly. Very much for the same reasons as for other requirements. And here's the thing: Personnel must also confirm reception and understanding of security policies and procedures, in a written format. They have to know what they're getting into, of sorts. Do you remember those Terms of Service that software forces you to accept, so that you prove that you've consented to how it can be used? Well, this is the equivalent for security policies in the organization. They have to mark them as "Read and Agreed". Then, 12.7 is screening potential personnel before hiring them. This is just running some checks to minimize the chances of an attack, due to internal employee action.

Hiring the wrong person. It may include background checks, criminal record checks, reference checks, and others on every person you hire. Even better would be to do these checks regularly, and not on hiring. Is it improbable that someone, that you've already hired, will become a criminal in the meantime? It is improbable. But is it impossible? It isn't. And if it happens, I bet you will want to know. Then, 12.8. Policies and procedures for service providers. This is because any service provider may compromise your card data in their services - whether they do hosting, physical storage, encryption of your data, or others. They are all potential weak links. So you must keep a list of all your service providers, as well as obtaining from each a written confirmation of their responsibility in safeguarding your card data.

By the way, if they refuse to provide this, something is wrong - this is actually required for them to be compliant with the PCI-DSS. It's literally the next sub-requirement! Also, you must necessarily have a process to select the service providers themselves. As well as yearly monitoring of their PCI-DSS compliance. Again, you don't need to have a specific process, just use common sense. As mentioned, 12.9 is the flip side of the previous one. If you are a service provider, you must confirm to your customers, in writing, that you are responsible for safeguarding their Cardholder Data (CHD). It's literally that point of the previous sub-requirement, but from the point of view of the service provider, and not the client. And the agreements may vary here.

Naturally. Depending on the services provided. But what's important is that the agreement itself must be enforceable - it must be valid and binding, and both parties must agree with that. Then, sub-requirement 12.10. Having an Incident Response (IR) plan. Look, in case of a breach, there must be a plan that dictates exactly what immediate actions will be taken. What happens if your firewall gets breached? What happens if your Intrusion Detection System (IDS) gets triggered? What happens if your File Integrity Monitoring (FIM) solution detects that a critical file has been changed? There must be immediate actions.

And, also, this plan must be reviewed yearly. For the same reasons as every other requirement of periodic updating. This Incident Response (IR) plan must include the roles, the responsibilities, the contact information of people, the recovery and continuity procedures, and possibly, data backups. Also, there must be personnel available 24/7. And, by the way, this is mandatory for you to be PCI-DSS compliant. It usually is a problem for smaller companies. Someone has to be available 24/7. In a large company, you can easily find someone. In a small company, it is harder. But it has to be done. You also need alerts from all types of systems, including your IDS or IPS, your firewall, your File Integrity Monitoring (FIM) solution, your logging systems, your antivirus, and so on.

And finally, changes to the Incident Response (IR) process - guess what - must follow a change management process themselves. Someone can't just change one of the steps "just because". Our final sub-requirement is 12.11, named "Quarterly service provider reviews". This is in case you are a service provider. And, again, because any intrusion doesn't just make you vulnerable - but all of your clients vulnerable as well - you must review your security procedures and policies quarterly, instead of yearly, like other organizations.

You also need additional controls to ensure that personnel are really following these.aAnd this includes reviewing different components, including: Your logs - remember, critical logs daily - your firewall rules, your procedures for configuration standards, your incident response procedures, and your change management processes for every single system. And especially those that deal with changes in configurations, such as changes in user credentials, changes to firewall rules, changes in the Intrusion Detection System (IDS), and so on. What are some examples of this requirement? The first is that it's a kind of policy consolidation.

As we mentioned, if you've noticed in the other requirements that final sub-requirement saying "document and enforce these procedures and policies" - our old friend, constantly popping up in every requirement - this is where they all come together. This requirement is not just the sum of the policies - but it is also the sum of the policies! Then, again, use common sense. Many of these policies, such as what's the acceptable use of technology, or how frequently to run background checks, don't need specific procedures - they just have to show that you put some thought into it. What the assessor will be looking for is, "Is there a specific reason behind this number, or is it here just because?". And if it's there "just because", you fail to comply.

And, finally, if there is no agreement, there's a problem. Specifically, I'm talking about that declaration, from a service provider, that they'll handle and safeguard your card data. It's required for them to provide this, to be PCI-DSS compliant. So, if they don't provide it - or if YOU don't provide it, as a service provider - that means that something's wrong here. Maybe they're lying, maybe they lost their compliance status, and they don't want to reveal it, or something else may be going on. But, usually, it's not anything good! What are the key takeaways from requirement 12? The first two requirements are about the policy and risks. 12.1 is about establishing, maintaining, and disseminating the policies to everyone involved. While 12.2 is about doing yearly risk assessment and evaluation.

Then, 12.3 is about usage policies. What technology can be used, for what purpose, what systems, and accessed by which roles? While 12.4 is about consolidating responsibilities. What does this person do? This person takes care of the firewall. This person takes care of the antivirus. And it goes all the way up to senior management. Then, 12.5 is the flip side. It's about assigning those responsibilities. Who's responsible for reviewing all logs? Who's responsible for reviewing all user credential changes? And so on, for every operation. 12.6 is about awareness. Making sure that employees, who are actually going to enact your security procedures, are, well, trained in information security! Then, the following two are about screening. 12.7 is about screening personnel, 12.8 is about screening providers.

12.7 is about doing background checks, criminal record checks, and so on, for the people you hire. While 12.8 is about having a process, and specific criteria for selecting your third parties - or for dropping them! As well as obtaining agreements from them, in terms of safeguarding your card data. Then, 12.9 is if you are a service provider, doing that yourself. Providing that same agreement to your clients. "I am responsible and will safeguard your card data". Then, 12.10 is about Incident Response (IR). There must be a protocol, it must include the key people, the key roles, their responsibilities, their contact information, there must be personnel available 24/7, there must be alerts from every critical system, and you must review this process yearly.

And, finally, 12.11 is, in case you are a service provider, review these procedures and policies quarterly. Remember, any vulnerability doesn't just affect you. - it affects your clients as well. So you can't just review these yearly, you have to do it quarterly. You are under more scrutiny, if you will. So you must review how security protocols are being followed - to firewall configurations, antivirus configurations, Incident Response procedures, change management for these, and others. Logs are even more frequent - daily. So, as we see, Requirement #12 is almost the bureaucratic part of the PCI-DSS. It's about documents, policies, processes, and more. It is the compilation of the "document and enforce" sub-requirements of all other requirements, but it even contains more areas, as you see, such as incident response, assigned owners, and more.

General Patterns and Recap

Let's talk about some general patterns of the 12 Requirements, and recap them again. So, we started with a shallow layer of all 12 requirements, then we went deep on every single one of them, and now I want to go back to that shallow layer, just to consolidate all that knowledge from those requirements. So let's take a look. Now that we're done with the 12 Requirements, let's take a moment to even try and recap everything that we've learned - as well as maybe draw some additional conclusions. So, first of all, we can detect some patterns across the different requirements. One - the documentation and enforcement of all policies and procedures. And this was for all areas.

From firewalls, to antiviruses, physical access, logical access, and everything else. What you do in terms of information security cannot be done informally. It must be a policy, and it must be put into practice. Then, another pattern that we saw were change management processes. That is, in order to effectively change something, a process must be followed - and we're talking about changes to developed applications, to user credentials, to firewall settings, or any type of configuration! Things can't just be changed unofficially. The third pattern that we saw was the use of common sense for certain definitions.

You don't need to do anything specific, you just need to do something that makes sense. What's the cryptoperiod for encryption keys? What are the periods for patching? For log review of non-critical logs? How frequently asset inventorying is done? What are considered significant changes to applications? Or what files and systems are considered "critical"? And so on. Remember, it's not so much about the specific values, it's just the fact that you've done your diligence. There is a reason for it. Even if it's basic. And, finally, another pattern was strong physical and logical security, at the end of the day.

Strong authentication, such as Multi Factor Authentication (MFA), strong encryption of data, keys, communication, and proper key management. So, state-of-the-art security in both domains. Let's quickly recap the 12 Requirements. The first was to keep a firewall. Having a proper firewall configuration, restricting unknown traffic, having a DMZ to isolate and triage traffic, having a firewall on all machines, and using change management for any changes in these. The second was about no defaults. Always changing default accounts and passwords, isolating servers and functionality, inventorying your assets - more as a signal than anything else - and removing all unneeded functionality. In other words, removing obvious vulnerabilities.

The third was to protect stored data. Limiting cardholder data storage to the essential, purging it, masking Personal Account Numbers (PANs) when stored or written down, as well as having proper key encryption and proper key lifecycle management. Cryptoperiod, key custodians, and maybe even split knowledge. The fourth requirement was about protecting transmitted data, including measures such as strong encryption - including for public wireless networks, or any other type of network, such as satellite, cellular, or others - as well as never sending plaintext Personal Account Numbers. The fifth requirement was about preventing malware.

Very simple. Have a proper antivirus solution that is regularly updated, performs regular scans, outputs regular logs, and that cannot be disabled by individual users. Then, requirement number six was to develop securely. Securing both off-the-shelf (OTS) software and your own developed software through patch installation - with the priority of these being defined by your periodic vulnerability assessments - but also including security requirements, themselves, in the Software

Development Lifecycle (SDLC) and properly training developers to address these vulnerabilities. Requirement 7 was about need-to-know access. The PoLP or the Principle of Least Privilege.

Defining user roles with the least privilege possible to perform their operations - usually based on their roles, or their job descriptions - and using some kind of access control mechanism, such as Active Directory, or an LDAP protocol for actual access control to systems and networks. Then, after limiting access, it's all about identifying access. Identifying specific users. Unique IDs, no shared users, strong authentication - whether passwords, objects, or biometric - having Multi Factor Authentication - so, two of these three methods - not sharing physical access control devices - so, user badges only used by their original user - strong password practices, including regular changes, automatic lockouts, and so on, and restricting actual databases to database admins.

Requirement #9 is the physical equivalent of 7. Restrict physical access. Having entry control on all rooms, distinguishing visitors - such as with color coding - authorizing those visitors, always accompanied and never alone, restricting actual physical access to media and locations with cardholder data (CHD), and having strict media storage, media distribution, and media destruction procedures. As well as employee training to prevent the tampering of devices. Number 10 was about monitoring networks. In other words, logging, logging, logging! First, having a logging solution.

Then, logging specific events - such as all admin operations, all operations on card data, all failed operations, and so on - logging specific data elements, such as the user, the type of operation, or the operation status (success or failure) - then, having one time sync for all logging systems, having File Integrity Monitoring (FIM) on logs, as well as backing them up as soon as possible, doing proper log retention

- 1 year for all logs, and 3 months immediately available - and immediately responding to log alerts. Requirement 11 was about testing regularly.

Vulnerability scanning, penetration testing - by an Approved Scanning Vendor (ASV), doing periodic AP identification - both legit AP and rogue ones, and what to do if you find the latter - regularly auditing all IPs as well, having an Intrusion Detection System (IDS) or Intrusion Prevention System (IPS), and having File Integrity Monitoring or change detection for all critical files. And, finally, requirement 12 was about having an information security policy. The sum of all policies, if you will! Technology usage policies, incident response policies, third-party service provider selection policies, risk assessment policies, employee screening policies, defining employee roles, responsibilities, and owners for tasks, employee awareness and employee training, among other elements.

In specific, Requirement #1 was about keeping a firewall. Protecting your Card Data Environment (CDE) from traffic. Both inbound and outbound. Also, having proper change management for these, as well as keeping documentation. It had 5 sub-requirements. Setting the configuration standards, based on the documentation - network topology, and card data flows - then, restricting connections between any untrusted network. Everything goes to the DMZ for triage, and only then, after authorized, does it go to your local networks. Then, prohibiting public direct access from the internet to the CDE, going through the DMZ, then installing firewall software on all portable computers accessing the Card Data Environment, and making sure that users can't remove it, and finally, documenting and enforcing all of these as procedures.

Requirement #2, about no defaults, was about minimizing obvious vulnerabilities. Remember, anybody can type the default password for any router, any hub, any operating system version, and they will find the defaults on the Internet in less than five seconds! It's about removing vulnerabilities as well - removing systems, ports, apps, anything you don't need, and that's just waiting to become a vulnerability. We had six sub-requirements. First, changing all defaults. Change default passwords, default users, default connection strings, encryption keys, everything else. Or, if you can't change it, disable it! Prevent the obvious vulnerabilities, one way or the other. Then 2.2, having configuration standards addressing these. Every time that you install a type of system, there must be a checklist, or procedure, saying "Remove this", "Isolate this system", "Don't place this in a server with this other functionality", and so on.

2.3, encrypting all admin access. Never using plaintext protocols. If you have a sniffer in your network, you don't want them to access admin credentials. 2.4, inventorying all assets in scope of PCI-DSS. Remember, it's more a signal than an actual practice. An assessor will know that a manager who knows their assets is probably protecting them. And the opposite also applies! If you don't even know what you have you're probably not securing it. 2.5 is our usual "document and enforce" requirement. All of this as written down procedures, and that employees actually use. Then, 2.6, only for service providers. If you are a shared service provider, making sure that one script, or app, or system, for one client, can't access another client's data. Requirement #3 was about protecting stored data. Making sure that cardholder data is properly protected.

Not just in terms of the encryption used - but also in terms of the encryption used! - but, besides that, properly managing the keys. Key management and key lifecycle. Also, protecting the Personal Account Numbers that are stored in excel sheets, emails, or on paper. Always encrypted or masked in some way. First, limiting storage or retention to the essential. Having data policies. Remember, the most secure way to store data is to never have to store it in the first place! Then, never storing Sensitive Authentication Data (SAD), such as the CVV number, or the PIN. Period. 3.3, masking stored Personal Account Numbers. There is no circumstance where you should show a full card number. Usually, you can show the first 6 digits, as well as the last 4. That's acceptable.

Then, rendering Personal Account Numbers unreadable on all communication channels. If an attacker obtains an excel sheet with card numbers, are they masked? Are they encrypted? Are they hashed? Or, on the other hand, are they in plaintext? That's what you don't want! Take your pick, just make them unreadable if they're intercepted. 3.5, encryption key protection. The keys used to encrypt card data must be in the least locations possible - and accessed by the least people possible. 3.6, procedures for encryption key management of those same keys. Having a cryptoperiod, key custodians, as well as procedures for what happens if a key is weakened, if it's compromised, or if it's expired. Then, finally, document and enforce all of these as policies and procedures.

Never informally. Requirement #4 was the counterpart of 3. The previous was to protect stored data, this one was to protect transmitted data. It's about maintaining cardholder data (CHD) secure while transmitting it - especially across public networks, which can be satellite, cellular, 802.11, or any other. And using best encryption practices for this. Also, never sending plaintext Personal Account Numbers internally, via SMS or email. It was relatively short. First, using strong encryption and security. Using a standard such as a NIST one, or the FIPS one, or an OWASP one - for example, WPA or WPA2 are acceptable, but not WEP. Or, in terms of algorithms, using one such as an AES - 128 or 256 or 3DES. 4.2, never sending unprotected Personal Account Numbers in instant messaging or email.

In other words, if an attacker is able to sniff one of your staff emails, it better not have full card numbers! Self-explanatory. And 4.3, document and enforce all of these. Requirement #5 was also relatively simple. Protect all systems against malware. It was about keeping an antivirus software to prevent malware on all machines that deal with cardholder data (CHD). Also very straightforward. 5.1, actually has anti-virus software! 5.2, frequently update the software, frequently run scans, and save the logs from those scans. Don't just have antivirus, actually use it! Third sub-requirement, never let the antivirus be disabled by individual users - unless it's an exception with a very good reason. And, finally, 5.4 - document and enforce all policies and procedures.

Requirement #6 was about secure development. In terms of securing both your developed and off-the-shelf software, by identifying vulnerabilities and patching them. Again, one of the most elusive requirements, because your developers probably care about functionality and not security! The sub-requirements included: First, vulnerability and risk ranking. Taking off-the-shelf (OTS) software, and your own, and ranking the possible vulnerabilities - which serves for the following sub-requirement, which is installing patches in a timely manner.

Critical vulnerabilities require patching within a month, while lower-priority vulnerabilities require patching between 2-3 months. Sub-requirement 6.3 was about having a secure software development lifecycle (SDLC). In short, including security requirements in the software requirements - and making sure that developers protect against common exploits. 6.4 was about change controls for your applications. In other words, analyzing the consequences of changes in your own software and rewriting security tests if they are significant changes, as well as allowing for rollbacks in case something goes wrong. 6.5 was about secure development training.

The only way to make sure that developers protect against common exploits is to explicitly train them on how to do it. 6.6 is about preventing public vulnerabilities. If you have public-facing applications, then you need to keep track of those vulnerabilities with a much higher frequency than for any other application. And 6.7 is our usual "document and enforce all of these procedures and policies". Requirement #7, about restricting access by need-to-know, was all about restricting access by employees, based on their roles. Again the Principle of Least Privilege (PoLP). The less permissions someone needs to have in order to do their job, they should have them. And no more than those. We have 3 straightforward sub-requirements for this requirement.

First, limiting cardholder data (CHD) in systems to the required individuals. If this person can have less access, then decrease it. If you can cut off their access even better! And this should be done by roles, which are associated with job descriptions. The second sub-requirement was to have a formal access control mechanism, to formalize this. Active Directory, LDAP, or any other. And, as usual, document and enforce all of these policies and procedures. Requirement #8, with the formal name of "Identifying and Authenticating Access to System Components", or in short, Identify Access, was about - unsurprisingly! - identification.

Making sure whoever authenticates for operations is who they say they are. There were several sub-requirements, but all of them were very direct. First, implementing identification management procedures. Unique IDs, automatic lockouts, automatic logouts, and so on. Then, strong authentication for all users. Passwords with strict standards, password management policies and identifying users before any major changes to credentials. The third element was demanding Multifactor Authentication (MFA) for all access to the Card Data Environment (CDE). It could be a combination of password and SMS, password and a physical device, or any other combination. 8.4 was our usual "document and enforce" requirement for these policies and practices.

Then, 8.5 no group IDs, no shared IDs... making sure every user performing operations is associated with one real-world person. After this, 8.6. Having individual physical security measures for each person. That means that nobody else can use your identity badge, for example. Whether with an automated or manual mechanism. 8.7, restricting Card Data Environment (CDE) database access to database admins. Everybody else has to use some kind of interface. Period. And finally, document and enforce all of these policies and procedures. Requirement #9 was about physical security. Restricting access to systems, rooms, physical media, and everything else in the real world dealing with Cardholder Data (CHD).

Again, we had a long list of sub-requirements, but all of them small and direct. First, enforcing entry controls. Cameras or access control for all rooms with cardholder data (CHD). 9.2, distinguish visitors. They must be identifiable from personnel - with a different color, for example - and have different access permissions. 9.3, restrict physical access. Whatever locations contain cardholder data (CHD) must be under lock and key. 9.4, authorizing visitors. Any visitor must be accompanied and they must have badges that clearly identify them. In other words, if they want to cause some trouble, it's not going to be easy! Also, keeping visitor logs, and requesting expired badges when they leave. 9.5 was about secure media storage.

Having them in locked rooms, with access control - possibly with biometric unlocking. And remember, this goes both for media, such as hard disks, and USB drives, but even printed cardholder data (CHD) records. Anything in the real world with card data. 9.6, distribute media securely. If you want to transport media with card data out of a room, there must be a process for it, management must be aware of it, and you have to track it, for example, if sent via mail. 9.7, strict media storage and accessibility. Have an inventory of the physical media so that you can know right away when something's missing or compromised. 9.8, securely destroy media.

Whatever media contain cardholder data (CHD), they must be destroyed securely - whether it's shredding, burning demagnetizing - but make sure to obtain a certificate. 9.9, especially protect devices that capture card data, such as POS devices, for example. Prevent tampering, for example, skimming, and make sure that personnel is trained to detect if they are tampered. 9.10 is to document and enforce all of these policies and procedures. Then, Requirement #10. Track and monitor access to networks. Or, with a shorter name, monitor networks. Or, with an even shorter name, log everything! Logging actions and identifying the root cause of attacks. It has 9 sub-requirements.

First, implement audit trails. In other words, have a logging solution. Second, specific events must be logged. All admin events, all intrusions, all failed operations, all operations on card data, and all operations that change user credentials. Then, which specific data to log for each event. The user, the operation type, the result (success or failure), the origination, and the element affected. 10.4, synchronize all clocks of all logging systems using one single source, so that you can easily reconcile the logs later. 10.5, prevent alteration of these logs. File Integrity Monitoring (FIM), to detect changes, and back them up - physically or digitally - as soon as possible. Get them in a secure area.

10.6, review logs frequently. Critical logs must be reviewed daily, other ones at a slower pace. 10.7 is simple. Keep all logs for one 1 total, while the last 3 months of that year must be immediately available in a local system or a local physical location. 10.8 is for service providers. If there is a failure in one of your critical systems, you have to detect it, and you have to report it right away - because it could affect your clients. 10.9 is documenting and enforcing all of these. The second to last requirement, Requirement #11 is about regular testing. Having processes and procedures to both detect and address the vulnerabilities you have. Sub-requirements include: First, frequently test and detect Access Points (APs).

Both legitimate ones and non-authorized ones. And have a procedure for what to do if you find the latter. 11.2, vulnerability scanning. Both internal and external. Knowing what you are exposed to. And done by an ASV, Approved Scanning Vendor. 11.3 takes it one step further: Penetration testing. Truly simulating how you would be attacked, with your specific circumstances. From the inside, from the outside, and from different layers. 11.4, very simple: Have an Intrusion Detection System (IDS) or Intrusion Prevention System (IPS). Keep it updated, and immediately react to any alerts. 11.5, use File Integrity Monitoring (FIM) of critical files. Make sure that no files are tampered with.

System files, files from critical systems that deal with Cardholder Data (CHD), and others that you may find important. And 11.6 demands the usual: None of these should be done informally, but they should be documented and enforced as policies and processes. The last requirement about maintaining an Information Security (InfoSec) policy, was the only management and not technology requirement. Keeping an Information Security policy at all levels of the organization, and it had 11 sub-requirements. First, establish, publish, maintain, and disseminate a policy. So, create that policy, keep it updated, and make sure that it reaches the people that it affects. 12.2, have an annual risk assessment process.

Every year, be aware of what threats and vulnerabilities you face and plan for them. 12.3, develop usage policies. What technology can be used, what technology can't be used, by whom, and what are the acceptable uses of those systems and devices. 12.4, there must be clear responsibilities. Whatever it is - firewall, antivirus, etc - there must be an owner. Period. 12.5 is about assigning said responsibilities. In the previous point, we said there must be an owner for these activities - and now we're saying, "Who is the owner?", for those activities. They must be identified. 12.6, security awareness. In other words, your personnel must know how important information security is from the moment they are hired. But also, being continually trained.

12.7, screen potential personnel before hiring them. Background checks, reference checks, criminal records, and others. If possible, even frequently, not just on hiring! If 12.7 is about screening your employees, 12.8 is about screening your service providers. Having a list of providers, what's the process for selecting a provider, and obtaining confirmation from them that they will safeguard your card data. 12.9 is in case YOU are a service provider. You must provide that confirmation to your clients. 12.10: Have an Incident Response (IR) plan. In case of a breach, what happens? Not only having it, but actually testing it every year.

Contacts, roles, responsibilities, continuity planning, backups, 24/7 people, and frequent alert review. And, finally, 12.11 is in case you are a service provider, and in that case, because your vulnerabilities affect your clients as well, you must review your Information Security policies quarterly instead of yearly - including incident response, firewall, antivirus, and all other critical components. What are some examples of general patterns in these requirements? The first is requirements 3 and 4. They can be considered parallels, in a way. Requirement 3 was about securing stored cardholder data (CHD) while Requirement 4 was about securing transmitted data.

Then, requirement 7 and 9. Requirement 7 was about protecting logical data, with need-to-know access, while Requirement 9 was about protecting access to physical data. But the philosophy is the same in both worlds! And, finally, Requirement 12, which was a full-spectrum Information Security (InfoSec) policy, and it could almost be considered the sum of all of the "document and enforce" points in all other requirements. What are our key takeaways? Well, they're one final review of all the requirements before we close the chapter! First requirement, have a firewall, to block unsecured traffic. Requirement 2 was about removing defaults to minimize obvious vulnerabilities.

Requirement #3 was about securing stored data, while Requirement 4 was about securing transmitted data, using a lot of principles in common. Strong encryption and protect anything that's in plaintext. Requirement 5 was about preventing malware by having antivirus, while Requirement 6 was about developing securely and identifying vulnerabilities - and actually patching them! - in both your applications and third-party applications as well. Requirement 7 was about limiting access to data through need-to-know policies, while Requirement 8 was about identifying access to those data. Unique IDs, strong authentication, and so on. Requirement 9 was the physical equivalent of 7.

Limiting physical access. Visitor management, physical media management, access control, and more. Requirement 10 was about monitoring - or logging. Logging events, logging specific data, and keeping log integrity. Requirement 11 was about regular testing. Both in terms of vulnerabilities in general, but also penetration testing, and ongoing protection, with an IDS or IPS, and also File Integrity Monitoring (FIM). And, finally, Requirement 12 was all about the policies. Making sure that people at all levels are aware of the information security policy. So, as you see, these are the 12 requirements, again, in a shallow, abridged version, just to help you consolidate all that deep knowledge.

We are now at the end of the 12 Requirements chapter, where we spent most of our time, and we covered, in detail, every single one of these requirements, as of version 3.2.1. Let's just cover all of the topics from this chapter, and consolidate our knowledge with some final questions. With this, we reach the end of the 12 Requirements chapter, where we covered each requirement of the PCI-DSS - version 3.2.1 - in detail. To properly cover the 12 requirements, we covered a total of 14 topics. First, we started with an overview of all 12 requirements.

Then, we jumped to Requirement #1: Having a firewall to protect your Card Data Environment. Requirement #2 was about removing defaults. Minimizing obvious vulnerabilities. Requirement #3: Protecting stored data. Encryption, masking, hashing, tokenizing, and other possible measures. Requirement #4 was about protecting transmitted data. Securing card data across public networks. Requirement #5: No malware. Having antivirus software, keeping it updated and keeping it running. Requirement #6 was about secure development. Making sure to identify and patch all vulnerabilities, as well as minimizing the vulnerabilities that you develop yourself internally.

Requirement #7: Need-to-know access. Limiting the people that deal with card data, and the permissions they have. Requirement #8: Identifying access. Unique IDs, no shared IDs, strong authentication, and other measures to tie every action to a user. Requirement #9: Restricting physical access. Protecting offices, rooms, physical media, identifying visitors, and having policies to store, move and destroy physical media - among others. Requirement #10 was about logging. Have logging software, log specific events, log specific data points within an event, keep time synchronized for all log solutions, have File Integrity Monitoring on the logs, as well as procedures to review them.

Requirement #11: Regular testing. Both internal and external testing, both vulnerability testing and penetration testing to prevent intrusions. Requirement #12 was about an information security policy. At all levels. Clear owners, roles, responsibilities, incident response, use of technology, third parties, employee screening, and other security measures. And then, we covered some general patterns of these 12 chapters, such as using common sense, documenting and enforcing everything, having change management for all changes, and others - as well as having recapped all 12 requirements.

Although this chapter was massive, and these questions don't even begin to cover the content, here are some questions that you can ask yourself to consolidate the knowledge of these 12 requirements, as of version 3.2.1 of the PCI-DSS: First, what are some examples of measures that must be taken to ensure strong cryptography? And I'm talking both about the types of algorithms, for example the standards, as well as practices for key protection and key management. Just name some of them. What are some examples of frequent code vulnerabilities that developers must protect against, when coding an application? What types of files should be subject to File Integrity Monitoring? Log files are obvious, but what about beyond those.

What's the policy for users to turn off their antivirus or firewall? What does the Principle of Least Privilege defend? How is it manifested in need-to-know access control, in Requirement 7, and physical access control, in Requirement 9? What two documents are crucial for firewall configuration? One related to the network and another related to the card data? What is the deadline to apply critical patches? What about the deadline for all other types of patches? With this, we reach the end of the 12 Requirements chapter, where we tried to cover every single one of these 12 requirements, how to comply with each one of these, and some best practices.

What Next

We are now at the end of the Fundamentals of PCI-DSS Book. Let's take a moment just to review the topics and chapters which we've covered. We are now at the end of the Fundamentals of PCI-DSS Book. In this Book, we had the goal of shedding light on the PCI-DSS framework. Both in general terms, but also in terms of the specific requirements. We touched on topics such as: What were the essential terms in the PCI-DSS? Such as the CDE, Card Data Environment, CHD, or Cardholder Data, SAD, or Sensitive Authentication Data, ROCs, which are Reports on Compliance versus the SAQs, or Self-Assessment Questionnaires, and a lot more.

Then, what were the 12 requirements, in detail, as well as the sub-requirements of every single one of these, which was the bulk of the Book, for sure. From firewalls, to antiviruses, to digital and physical access control, strong encryption in storage and transit, and many others. Also, we covered a brief history of the PCI-DSS framework and versions. And we also touched on how the assessment process works, itself, with Reports on Compliance and Self-Assessment Questionnaires, as well as the 8 types of SAQs, depending on the type of merchant. In this Book, we covered 2 main chapters.

First, we covered the essentials of the PCI-DSS. This is where we talked about the framework in an introductory manner. Its history, the key terms, the assessment process, and more. Then, we covered the 12 requirements in detail. The absolute majority of the time of this Book, for sure. Every single one of the sub-requirements, including the procedures and policies of each. With this, we close the Fundamentals of PCI-DSS chapter. Thank you so much for reading this Book. I sincerely hope it has helped you professionally. And with this, we close the Fundamentals of PCI-DSS Book. Thank you so much for reading.

Capital Market Fundamentals

Hello and welcome to Capital Market Fundamentals. So what would you get out of this Book? First, you will gain fundamental knowledge of capital markets. Then you will also learn the basics of fundamental technical and sentimental analysis. You also learn what is about relatives and the bonds. Lastly, you also get a list of very powerful tools for all of your investment analysis needs. That is right. All of these are really, really powerful tools that you can get for free with no sign ups at all. This Book is for people who are looking for knowledge in capital market basics, as well as people who want an introduction to the topic of technical and fundamental analysis.

Lastly, this Book is for people who want to access free, powerful analysis tools with no need to sign up in order to maximize their investment gains. So let us now go over the Book outline. We will kick start this Book with the capital market and the stock markets chapter. We will start off with a video talking about our capital markets. We will then move on to a description about the stock market, as well as videos about fundamental analysis and technical analysis. We will then move on to the derivatives and bonds, a chapter in this chapter. I will touch base about the different instruments that you will find within derivatives, as well as what exactly bonds are.

Lastly, I will go over the segment called Other Topics in which I will talk about IPO valuation, market sentiment. And Of course, one of the most important parts of this Book, I look over a list of the tools for market analysis that is completely free with no sign up whatsoever. And they are absolutely powerful to maximize your return of investment. Well, I hope that you will learn a lot from this Book. And I hope that the tools that I give you in this Book will provide you with a lot of the assets that you need to maximize your investments. Thank you. And I'll see you in the next video.

What Are Capital Markets

So now let us start off this Book with what are actually capital markets now. It is through capital markets that savings and investments are routed between those in need and those who have money to lend or invest. Banks and investors are typical suppliers of money, whereas enterprises, governments and individuals are the typical consumers of money or capital. In this sense markets for primary and secondary securities exist with the stock market and the bond market being the two most prevailing financial markets under the umbrella of capital markets. And the purpose of the capital market is to link together potential suppliers with potential investors in order to trade securities.

When you hear the word capital markets, you're probably thinking of a location where a variety of companies exchange financial products. Some of these venues may include the stock market, the bond market, the currency and foreign exchange markets, among others. New York, London, Singapore and Hong Kong are among the main financial centers of which these markets are situated in. Suppliers and consumers of funds make up the capital markets. Financial organizations, pension funds and life insurance companies are among the sources of cash in these markets. Home and auto buyers and non-financial enterprises and governments that are in need of funding infrastructure investment and operational expenditures are among the consumers of the capital market.

Equities and DEP securities are sold on these capital markets. They're also known as stocks or ownership stakes in a firm. On the other hand, IOUs with interest are kind of depth securities in which one of the most popular examples are bonds. And they're also part of the capital market as well. It is essential for the contemporary economy to have a functional capital market which is responsible for moving money from those who have to those who need it. Capital market has two big components, namely the primary and the secondary market. Primary and secondary markets rely on computer based electronic platforms for the maturity of their transactions.

Let us start with the primary market, a business where shares can only be purchased on the primary market by specified investors who purchased the securities directly from company companies that go public, offering their stocks and bonds to large institutional investors, such as hedge funds and mutual funds in order to raise cash. These are also known as initial public offerings, and are commonly known as IPOs in primary capital markets. Companies go directly to investors and utilize their money to invest in assets such as buildings, plants, machinery, etc.

Financing from financial institutions is excluded from the primary market, since issuing a loan from a financial institution involves turning private money into public capital, which this process isn't known as becoming public. Equity shares, debentures bonds, preference shares and other innovative instruments are some of the common securities offered in the primary market. Now, there are four ways that securities can be issued in the primary market, and they are first through prospectus, second offering sale, third issue, new shares, and for private placement. Let's start off with the first way, which is through prospectus with this method.

Company releases a prospectus to enlighten and entice the public. The company offers facts about why funds are being raised. Previous financial performance history and the future prospects of the company in the prospectus. Investors can determine whether or not to invest in the firm based on the prospectus information regarding risks and earning possibilities through the IPO. A firm may reach out to a huge number of people and the general public. Bankers, brokers and underwriters are often used by corporations to obtain funds from the general public. Now the second way is called offer shares. With this, a middleman who buys a large number of securities from a firm makes additional securities available to the public, but not directly from the company.

Brokerage firms are the most common middlemen in this case. The stocks are then sold in two stages, the first stage is when the firm issues them to an intermediary at face value. And at the second stage is when the intermediary sells them to a broader public at a higher price to make profit. The company can avoid the procedures and the complexity of offering securities directly to the public by using this technique. Now, the third way is the issue for new shares, and this is to existing shareholders mostly here. Fresh shares are issued to current owners, as the name implies.

Shareholders have to write a first refusal and must be offered a fresh issue before it is made available to outsiders in proportion to their existing holdings. Each shareholder has the option of purchasing more stock. Current corporations are not allowed to issue shares without first granting pre-emptive rights to existing shareholders, because if new shares are offered to new new shareholders, the current equity holders may lose their part in capital and control of the company because this would in turn dilute their ownership. Preemptive or right issues are necessary for established companies to stop this. Lastly, there's also what we call private placement.

This involves selling securities to an intermediary at a set price, who then sells them to Chozen clients at a higher price in a second stage. As a result of the prospectus, reputable clients prefer to acquire the securities through an intermediary. These securities are issued to chosen clients such as Utti LLC and General Insurance using this technique of distribution. It is a cost effective technique, as the business does not have to pay underwriter fees, managers cost agents fees or to put its name on the stock exchange, since they cannot afford to acquire money through a public offering. A lot of small and fledgling companies choose private placement as their way to tap into the primary market space.

In a secondary market, what it has are securities that have already been issued or that have been previously owned for which it can be sold or purchased as opposed to the primary market. The secondary market is where securities are sold by companies directly to their investors and where existing investors sell the securities to new investors. The investor may be in need of cash. While another investor may wish to purchase the business of shares because he is unable to obtain them directly from the company in the secondary market. Both investors can meet and trade securities for cash through a broker due to the fact that securities are only purchased and sold between investors.

There is no capital formation in the secondary market. However, the secondary market indirectly helps capital formation by providing liquidity for the company stock. As a result, investors would have to wait until the end of the redemption period or the company's dissolution to get their money back. However, with the presence of a secondary market, investors can convert the securities into cash whenever they want it. And it also gives them the opportunity to make money as securities are traded on the secondary market. Investors have a short term investment horizon, and can take advantage of the secondary markets. Liquidity by buying and selling assets at their convenience or stock exchanges are considered examples of secondary markets.

Stock Market

A stock market is a type of designated market where you may trade various types of securities in a controlled, secure and monitored setting. The stock market promotes fair pricing procedures and transaction transparency by bringing together hundreds of thousands of market participants who want to purchase and sell shares. Unlike older stock markets, which used paper based physical share certificates to issue and trade, today's computer aided stock exchanges function entirely electronically. Stock markets provide a safe and a regulated environment in which market participants may confidently trade shares and other qualifying financial products with zero to minimal operational risk. The stock markets operate as primary and secondary markets in accordance with the regulations set forth by the regulator.

The stock market, when acting as a primary market, permits firms to issue and sell the shares to the general public for the first time through initial public offerings or IPOs. This practices eight businesses in obtaining the cash they want from investors. It basically implies that a corporation splits itself into a number of shares and sells a portion of those shares to the general public at a price. A company will require a marketplace where these shares may be sold to make this process easier, which the stock market provides within this marketplace. If all goes according to plan, the business will be able to sell a part of the company ownership to get the funding it needs. In return, investors will get shares from the company, which they may expect to keep for the length of their choice in the hopes of a rising share price and potential dividend payments.

The stock market functions as a facilitator for this capital raising process, receiving a fee from the company and its financial partners in exchange for its services following the initial public offering or IPO. The stock market also acts as a trading platform for regular buying and selling of the listed shares, which is called the secondary market. Every deal that takes place on the stock exchanges platform during secondary market activity pays the stock exchange a fee. In such trading operations, the stock exchange is responsible for guaranteeing price transparency, liquidity, price discovery and fair transactions.

The exchange maintains trading systems that efficiently manage to buy and sell orders from diverse market participants as nearly all major stock exchanges across the world now function electronically. They provide the price matching function to help buyers and sellers execute trades at a price that is fair to both parties. At a later date, a publicly traded business may offer fresh more shares through other means, such as a rights issue or follow-on offer. They would even have the ability to repurchase or delist their stock. Such traits are made possible by the stock market.

The stock exchange frequently produces and maintains different market level and sector specific indices, such as the S&P 500 Index or the NASDAQ index to track the overall market's behavior. All business news announcements and financial reporting are also maintained by the stock exchange, and are typically found on their official websites. A stock market also facilitates a variety of other transaction related operations at the company level. Profitable firms, for example, may pay dividends to investors, which are generally derived from a portion of the company's earnings. The exchange keeps track of all of this data and can help with its processing to some extent.

So now let us go over some of the primary purposes of a stock market. The first function of a stock market is to have fair dealings and securities transactions. Now the stock exchange must guarantee that all interested market players have rapid access to data for all buy and sell orders. Therefore, assisting an affair into transparent pricing of securities based on conventional demand and supply criteria is essential. It should also be capable of efficiently matching relevant buy and sell orders. The second function for the stock market is to have price discovery in an efficient way. The act of determining the correct price of a security is generally accomplished by analyzing market supply and demand, as well as other aspects connected with the transactions.

And stock markets must provide an effective system for price discovery. The third function of a stock market is maintaining liquidity, while the quantity of buyers and sellers for a certain financial security is really out of the stock market's control and must ensure that everyone who is eligible and wants to trade has immediate access to place orders that are executed at a fair price. The four functions of a stock market is to maintain transaction security and validity, while additional players are beneficial to market efficiency, the same market must also guarantee that all participants are verified and adhere to the essential rules and regulations, leaving no space for any of the parties to fail.

You should also guarantee that all linked businesses operating in a market must follow the rules and act within the legal framework established by its regulators. Lastly, the fifth function for the stock market is to protect investors along with rich and institutional investors. The stock market also serves a significant number of small investors who have little amounts of money to invest. These investors may have inadequate financial understanding and be unaware of the risks associated with investing in stocks and other publicly traded securities. The stock exchange must take the appropriate steps to guarantee that such investors are also protected from financial loss and that consumer trust must be maintained.

A company's worth and consequently the value of its shares can be determined in a variety of ways. Looking at a company's market value, also what we called that market capitalization is the simplest fundamental approach to determine its worth. Market capitalization is simply the amount obtained by multiplying the price of a single share, but the total number of outstanding shares of a stock calculating the market capitalization is simple. It is the current share price multiplied by the number of outstanding shares. So, for example, the market valuation of a firm with one million shares outstanding and a share price of five dollars per share is going to be five million dollars.

There are five basic stock market capitalization categories, and they are the market cap. Small cap, mid-cap, large cap and ultra cap. Let's start with microcaps. These companies have a market capitalization of under two hundred and fifty million dollars and that they are pretty much the teeniest, tiniest and hence riskiest equities accessible in the stock market. Next goes to small cap, where the market cap is between two hundred and fifty million to one billion dollars. They outperform microcaps, and yet they still have plenty of room for development and growth. So many people are actually interested in investing in small caps.

Now, for many investors, the mid-cap category, which is between one billion dollars to five billion dollars, is a reasonable balance between tiny and the large companies. These companies offer some of the protection of large caps while also offering some of the potential growth of small caps. So they're actually the middle of everything. So they got a good balance of growth and security at the same time. Moving on to the fourth category is the large cap, which has a market capitalization between five billion dollars to twenty five billion dollars. This group is often designated for cautious stock investors seeking consistent growth while maintaining a higher level of safety. Blue chips are terms used to describe stocks in this group.

Lastly, we have what we call the ultra cap or the ultra cap, which has a market cap of more than twenty five billion dollars. These caps are also known as mega caps, and they clearly relate to the biggest of the huge just companies in the stock market that you would see in the world. The examples include companies like General Electric, the company size and market are very important in terms of looking at the safety of your investment. Large cap stocks are regarded as safer than small cap equities when all other factors are equal. Small cap stocks, on the other hand, have a higher growth potential so determined by your appetite for risk.

You could invest in smaller capitalization investments, but if you want to keep on the safe side, you should have it in your investment situated mostly in mid-cap or larger. Now, if you are in terms of even having a very low appetite of risk, even for a large, large cap stock, what I would advise you to look at is something called an index. An index is a standardized means of tracking the performance of a collection of assets. Indexes are used to track the performance of a group of securities designed to mirror a specific market segment. An example of an index is the Standard and Poor's 500 index, which is more commonly known as the S&P 500 financial or economic statistics such as interest rates, inflation or industrial production are measured using indices.

Indexes are frequently used as benchmarks for evaluating the performance of a portfolio's return. Indexing is a common investment technique that aims to passively duplicate a market index rather than aiming to exceed it. Each stock and bond market index has its unique technique for computation. In most situations, the index is relative. Change is more essential than the quantitative number that represents it. Investors must look at the amount that their index has changed, which is frequently stated as a percentage to see how the index has moved from the previous day. The term indexing refers to a type of passive fund management, instead of actively stock picking and market timing, that is deciding which securities to invest in and when to purchase and sell them. A fund portfolio manager constructs a portfolio that mirrors the stocks in a particular index.

Index funds were designed to monitor the performance of indexes because you can't invest directly in them. These funds include assets that closely resemble those contained in an index, allowing investors to wager on the indexes performance in exchange for a fee. Now, if you're not investing in index funds, you probably need to do homework for the stocks that you want to buy yourself. With that, there are three types of analysis for stocks, and they are fundamental analysis, technical analysis and sentiment analysis. Let us explore each one of these in this Book.

Fundamental Analysis

All publicly listed firms, as well as those that receive public investment money, are obligated to report their operations. Companies must tell investors what they are made of. But unfortunately, all of the information investors need to know about a firm does not fit into an easy to read format. Instead, a succession of financial statements and other sources of basic data break down the main parts that describe a company in great detail. The most basic aim of fundamental analysis is to read these essential financial documents and get insights from them. Fundamental analysis is the ability to look through all the information provided by companies in order to make informed judgments.

So why bother with technical terms like net income or discounted cash flow analysis when you can just switch on the television? Shoot down a few stock symbols by the stocks and hope for the best. Furthermore, isn't knowing how businesses function a waste of time after all? Stock market is just like betting on a company and hoping for the best, right? Or isn't? Just allow. Following the overall trend is good enough. Like a bull market will result in everything going up and a bear market will result in everything going down. Right. Also, aren't there a lot of podcasts, YouTube videos, TV shows, etc. that provide all the homework analysis for you anyways? So why bother now investing in visas on the Internet and media? Believe it or not, it can be full of BS.

There's always a new financial guru or economist who comes up with a fresh strategy for picking successful stocks. And so effective stock selection frequently boils down to basic analysis instead of relying on the stock predictions that you hear. And that is when fundamental analysis comes into play. So what are the benefits of doing fundamental analysis? Well, there are three benefits, and they are that company valuation assesses the health of a company and that it is based on facts rather than speculation. A subjectively valued asset's price is usually determined by what someone else is willing to pay for the stock market, which functions as an auction between buyers and sellers.

Does an excellent job of putting a price tag on a business's fundamental analysis. On the other hand, provide another method to assess how much investors are paying for a company when they purchase or sell it, and whether or not the price is worth it. The fundamental analysis will review you as to whether growth is continuing or will start to decline. There will be hints if you know where to look as to when should be a good time to sell the stock. Because companies are obligated to disclose a central part of their operations. A fundamental nout analyst will frequently be the first to notice whether or not there's a problem. Now, lastly, it is easy to get caught up in broad excitement for a company's mission or the new product that it sells.

After all, CEOs are always very charming in their speech. Fundamental analysis blinds you to the investing hoopla that these CEOs boast about in their official statements and focuses you on cold, hard facts of business rather than the hype that they try to stir. With fundamental analysis, there are three main documents that you need to look at for information, and they are the income statement balance sheet and the cash flow statements. Let us first start with the income statement. When you acquire shares in a company, you're generally not doing so to help the company. You're buying a piece of the company's future income and profits when you buy the stocks.

If all goes well, their business will expand and your investments will increase in value. The trick is to ensure that the firm keeps its part of the deal by producing profit. The income statement is the document that you need for this information. Companies that have issued shares on the stock exchange, such as the Nasdaq, must file an income statement. The income statement describes the company's performance in great detail for each quarter and year. Fundamental analysis necessitates paying close attention to the income statement for any indication that the firm isn't advancing as it should be. Or, alternatively, is performing better than as expected. There are no two income statements that appear the same and small variances can make comparing one company's income statement to another difficult. Income statements can also differ based on a company's area of operation.

Fortunately for investors, accountants have standardized a manner in which firms must compile their income statements. The basic structure of income statements is more or less usually the same. The components that make up the basic framework of an income statement would include first the revenue, which is the amount of money the firm made by selling goods and services. Second, it is the cost of goods sold. To make money, you have to spend money. The cost of goods sold is the amount of money spent by a firm to generate the product or service that is sold. These are direct costs, which means they are expenses for goods that might be used to make the products.

For many manufacturing firms, the cost of products sold is the most significant single expense of conducting business. Then the third thing would be operating expense companies incur indirect expenses while they do business. But they may not go directly into the product. These expenses are typically essential or significant, yet they're in debt, yet they're indirectly accounted to the operation of the of the of creating the product itself, operating expenditures or overhead, as it is more often called in management accounting. Are the names given to these indirect costs and include things such as marketing, admin and research and development costs? The fourth component is other income. Businesses can earn money from sources other than selling their normal goods and services.

For example, selling an asset such as equipment is one of them. The fifth part, Of course, is other income. There's also other expenses. Now, this includes other costs that do not count as normal operating expenses, and some of the examples include paying severance to laid off staff or depreciation of specific assets. Now, six components in which it is actually calculated from the first five components are actually the earnings before interest and tax, which is short form as . This is what's left after subtracting the cost of goods sold. Operating expenditures and other expenses from revenue. Now, Of course, after because it is before interest and tax. The next two components are interest expense and taxes.

Now, the majority of businesses borrow money to support the operations or purchase inventory, and the company needs to review how much it pays in interest to borrow money in the interest chapter. As for taxes, well, the company needs to review how much they paid the government in terms of taxes. Simply put. Now, what is left is going to be a net income. So with you minus the interest expense and then you minus the tax. And what it comes off to is what it's called the net income. And based on accounting regulations or GAAP, this is basically how much the Pistons earned during the time. So let us talk about the first component, because this is actually really important, which is revenue.

Revenue is a crucial statistic for a fundamental analyst reviewing an income statement since it shows you whether the company is growing or shrinking and the demand for their businesses when comparing revenue earned over the Book of a year or quarter to revenue recorded during the same time the previous year. The results can be rather informative for us. This easy comparison shows if the company's growth is either increasing or decreasing. Furthermore, companies in short boast about how well-liked their products and services are. However, revenue is where the hype can be measured. Even if the company's costs are out of line and it's still losing money. Strong demand for products will show up in the revenue.

Furthermore, you can benchmark a company's revenue against its competitors. While there are numerous methods to determine the size of a business such as the number of workers, revenue is a very good indicator when determining which company is the largest in a competitive industry. Revenue should always come first. And your analysis? Unfortunately, companies have a lot of flexibility in how and when they record or recognize revenue under accounting regulations. The most common type of distortion occurs when a firm records revenue before a consumer buys or receives a product. And as a result, regulators frequently advise companies to be extra cautious while booking revenue, as more than a third of misstated financial statements were due to incorrect revenue recognition.

The majority of businesses will have several revenue line items in most cases. There will be a total revenue line that adds all the money received from all of the company's business units. However, if the firm is complicated, overall revenue may be broken down into its component pieces so it can determine which units are performing the best. Analyzing the breakdown of revenue numbers would allow one to analyze the diversity of income streams of the business, as well as which of their income streams are most important for the business. Companies must keep up things such as rising raw material prices by generating income, other by raising pricing or by developing new goods with larger price tags.

Even if you're merely looking for a steady return in a mature industry, you want to see revenue grow over time to maintain the company's profitability in line with inflation. So what do you need to do, analysis on the revenue items? Well, to put it simply, we need to get the historical revenue and calculate the percentage change over a year to year if the percentage change increases over the years. It means that it is growing. But if the percentage change is getting lower or dips to negative, it is shrinking. All businesses have costs. Direct expenses, such as raw materials and indirect costs such as overhead and advertising consume a significant part of income.

All of these expenses are reflected in the income statement so that investors can understand how much a firm spent on revenue generation. While some investors focus just on overall expenditures or examine cost of goods sold and operational expenses, delving deeper into the cost details yields much more insight. Fundamentals and analysts use an effective approach to analyze cost details. And it is what we call the common approach. Common sizing is a process of measuring the size of lines on financial statements by comparing them to a total, you compare each cost to revenue. When you apply common sizing to the income statement in that manner, you can quickly observe whether the company's costs are increasing at an alarming rate in comparison to the company's growth.

The best part is that common sizing is straightforward to turn the amount into percentage. Just divide each cost by total revenue and multiply it by a hundred. Now, it is typically better to utilize any years of data when common sizing and income statements so we can observe the changes from year to year. You will notice a pattern if, for example, a company's admin expenditure is increasing often and out of ordinary blip on the common sizing analysis indicates something worth investigating further. The company's net profit is what remains after all bills have been paid, including all direct expenditures, operational expenses and taxes.

This is what we call the net income. And the formula for this is net income equals revenue, minus cost of goods sold, minus operating expenses, plus other income, minus other expenses, minus interest expenses, minus taxes. For many investors, net income is the be all and end all. It is the figure used to compare a company's performance to previous years and to investor expectations. You will want to observe how quickly net income increased or decreased in comparison to past years. Mashing up or combining various indicators is a fantastic approach to gain insights in fundamental research. Here's an excellent example. Combine your knowledge of net income with your newly acquired ability to compute growth.

If a company's net income grows more slowly than it sells, it's a good indication that its costs are out of control. Calculating the year over year percentage changes for revenue and net income is an effective approach to assess how net income compares to revenue. For example, you can easily observe how effectively the firm is controlling expenses when demand for its products increases and decreases. By comparing sales and net income growth. Profit margin analysis is one of the most effective techniques to estimate a company's profit, a profit margin at its most basic level is the amount of money left over after all of a company's expenditures have been paid. Profit margins may be measured in a variety of methods, all of which are useful in fundamental analysis.

There are three types of profit margins that are important, and they are gross profit, operating profit and net profit margin. One of the easiest methods to look at profitability is to look at a company's gross profit, also known as gross margin. After removing direct cost, also known as cost of goods sold, gross profit is what's left. Gross profit is a matter of money. A firm makes after paying all of the costs that are directly associated with manufacturing the product. On the other hand, the operating profit margin of a company takes into account more cost, and the gross profit margin operating profit margin takes into account not just the company's direct costs, but also its indirect costs. After removing overhead expenditures and cost of goods sold.

Operating profit margin is what's left saving the best for last. The most complete measure of profitability is the company's net profit margin, or in other sense, what I previously talked about as net income. The term net profit refers to the amount of money left over. After all, expenditures and expenses have been paid. Now I have to look at the income statement. The second document that we need to look at is the balance sheet. The balance sheet contains information about companies assets, liabilities and shareholders equity. It is used to calculate rates of return and evaluate a company's capital structure, their financial statements that show what business owns and has to pay together with the amount of money invested by the company stockholders.

The balance sheet is a snapshot of a company's financial situation at a certain point in time. They are used best by comparing historical balance sheets to see the changes in assets and liabilities, as well as benchmarking against its competitors to see its performance. So what gives the balance sheet its name? Well, a balance sheet is set to be balanced in that the value of the assets should equal to the sum of liabilities and stockholders equity. Let us start with a talk about what are the assets in the balance sheets. A company's assets can be divided into current assets and noncurrent assets. Current assets are those that will or should be converted into cash within the next 12 months. Naturally, cash on hand and inventory are the most frequent current assets.

Receivables are another type in which there are short term loans that a form extends to its clients. Noncurrent assets on the other end are assets that cannot be turned into cash over the next 12 months. Fixed assets include equipment that are needed in the operation of a business. Furniture and fixtures, as well as any real estate in the business. Among others are considered non current assets. After looking at assets, Nix's liabilities are debts owed by the company. Again, it is split by current obligations or current liabilities and noncurrent liabilities, which is quite similarly structured as assets. Financial commitments that must be paid within the next 12 months are known as current liabilities, customers, account payable, company line of credit. And the current part of long term debt are among the most prevalent examples of current liabilities and businesses.

Their short term liabilities, as they are typically paid within 30 to 60 days after the day a product is delivered or service is performed. As for noncurrent liabilities, they're more or less the long term debt that the business has. The third and last part is the stockholders equity in a company's balance sheet. Stockholders equity consists of share capital plus retained earnings. Aside from that is a measure of the residual worth of assets, less liabilities that satisfies the balance formula of the balance sheet. There are four major components to the stockholders equity, and they are the share capital retained earnings.

Net income and dividends. The amount obtained by the reporting business through transactions with shareholders is referred to as shared capital in general. Companies can issue either ordinary or preferred stock when a corporation is liquidated or dividends are paid. Ordinary shares are paid only after preferred shareholders have been compensated. Businesses profits are not paid to shareholders as dividends, but instead invested back into the firm are known as retained earnings. Other uses for retained earnings include fixed asset acquisitions and debt servicing. Now, Of course, as I mentioned earlier, the difference is what you paid to shareholders periodically.

And lastly, Of course, net income is what you have from the income statement. Analysis is very similar, in which we can use the common approach to gain insight on the individual items and see how it is benchmark with other competitors, as well as the performance of the business itself over several years. Companies are often judged on their ability to generate enough cash to fulfill their debt commitments and cover their operational expenditures. Which is why we need the third document, the cash flow statement. The cash flow statement is a financial statement that details how much cash and cash equivalents enter and leave a business with the cash flow statement.

Investors can see how a company's operations are handled, where its money comes from, and how it spends money. Investors who use this document to assess whether a firm is financially sound. As for the components to the cash flow statement, there are three types of activities, and they are the operating activities, investing activities and the financing activities. Cash from operating activities shows how much money a firm generates from its products or services. Cash for investing activities are activities with the intention of generating a return in the future. A few examples of this type of activity are capital expenditures. Lending money and the selling of securities.

Lastly, in a company's cash flow statement, cash flow from financing activities is a part that indicates the net net cash flow from funding the company by lenders and investors. Debt equity and dividends are all types of financing operations that can be performed and are part of the financing activities within the cash flow statement. A company's fundamentals can be reviewed efficiently with the use of financial ratios in fundamental analysis. Financial ratios are useful since they allow you to compare the financials of different firms and get fast insights on what's going on. Financial ratios often fall into one of five categories, which are the ones shown in front of you right now. And they are profitability, leverage, efficiency, condition and of valuation. Let us look at the first type of ratios, which is profitability.

These ratios help you to put a company's profit or loss into context in the business world. These ratios are sometimes referred to as profit margins. Ratios that belong to the profitability group include gross margin ratio, which is equal to gross profit. Divide by net sales, operating margin ratio, which is equal to operating income, divided by net sales, and return on asset ratio, which is equal to net income, divided by total assets. Next is leverage. This basically tells you how much of the company operation comes from. Depth ratios belonging in this category include the debt ratio, which is the total liabilities divided by total assets, the debt to equity ratio, which is equal to total liabilities developed by shareholders, equity and interest coverage ratio, which is equal to operating income divided by interest expense.

Now, the interest coverage ratio basically tells you how easily a company can pay off its interest. Next comes the efficiency ratio, which allows you to gauge how good the company is managing its resources. The ratio under this category includes the asset turnover ratio, which is equal to the net sales divided by average total assets. The inventory turnover ratio, which is equal to cost of goods sold divided by average inventory and the day's sales and inventory ratio, which is equal to three hundred sixty five, divided by the inventory turnover ratio. On this day, sales and inventory ratio tells you how many days the company holds onto inventory before a sale is made. As for the condition category, it provides insight as to the likelihood that the company can endure the bad times.

Ratios under this category include the current ratio, which is equal to the current assets divided by current liabilities. The acid test ratio, which is equal to the current asset minus inventory divided by the current liabilities and the cash ratio, which is the cash and cash equivalent of by current liabilities. Now, the asset test ratio is the company's ability to pay off short term liabilities with quick assets. Lastly, the devaluation category allows one to assess what is the overall value of the stock and whether or not it is worth it.

The ratio under this category includes the book value per share ratio, which is shareholders equity minus preferred equity divided by the total common shares outstanding. The dividend yield ratio, which is equal to the dividend per share, divided by share price to earnings per share ratio, which is net earnings divided by total shares outstanding. And the price to earnings ratio, which is equal to the share price divided by the earnings per share.

Technical Analysis

Technical analysis is the study of how security prices move and how to profit from this knowledge while avoiding losses trading in a technical manner is what we call opportunistic. What this entails is to anticipate the price of the assets over a future time period so that you may purchase and sell it for profit. The goal of technical analysis is to earn money from trading, not to think of holding a security as a way to save money. And as a result, technical analysis requires a more aggressive trading approach than fundamental analysis. The most common blunder made by new technical traders is putting too much faith in technical approaches in terms of dependability and accuracy.

Technical traders with a lot of experience realized that no strategy works 100 percent of the time. Many strategies, in fact, only succeed when the vast majority of market players believe they will, creating a self-fulfilling prophecy. You don't need to know whether a technological hypothesis is scientifically verifiable as long as you can determine which one is capturing the market's interest at any given time. Understanding that no approach works 100 percent of the time helps you counter detractors' claims. The technical analysis as a whole is worthless since techniques aren't 100 percent dependable.

The fact that a method doesn't always work isn't the proper criterion for judging it. In the end, the usefulness of an analytical approach in financial markets is measured by whether it allows you to regularly make more money than you lose. Technical analysis, it's the skill of observing crowd behavior in order to join them and benefit from their momentum. For example, when a new piece of information is released and is interpreted favorably by many traders or a few large companies or large news companies are posting it, the price will climb. Current.

Contrastingly, when everyone else is selling, you should as well, because overall going off, the flow pays off.

Market participants, like any other human beings, tend to behave in predictable ways in what we call a mania. People become irresponsible and irrational, and when a bubble ruptures makes them extremely wary, causing them to become overly cautious, which in this situation, we turn from what we call mania to a panic situation. This occurs when traders acquire a product of security without consideration to its intrinsic worth, or whether they'll be able to sell it later on for more money. They are afraid of missing out on a chance. They're caught up in the moment and unreasonable for a short time because of this. And as a result, panic sets in and individuals are forced to accept ever lower prices simply to get any money back, if at all.

There are just a few instances in economic history when a mania or a panic occurs, but this occurs quite often in the world of technical analysis. As a result of emotional peaks and valleys, price spikes occur on a daily, weekly or even on an hourly basis. They may not be utilized in technical trading jargon. But the emotion and price consequences are identical to those of manias and panics in a macro economic sense. Now, why is that? Well, individuals behave differently from others in a crowd. There are many types of crowds, fraternity sport teams, social groups, religious sects, etc., etc. And the list is endless.

Each individual in a crowd adds up to a whole and one in a crowd. Even the most rational people may behave in the most bizarre of ways. Technical trader wants to be aware of what the crowd is doing, but without falling to its own irrational whims and desires. It takes a lot of effort for technical traders to ignore, to talk about securities, especially if it comes from specialists or, you know, the TV experts, for instance, or the podcast experts on what the next stock to buy. As a result, you may suffer from information overload, as well as information misinformation if you rely too much on those so-called experts. Now, the price contains all the information you need to make a trading choice.

And there are several advantages to looking at pricing rather than speculating on what others would believe based on what they've heard. And as such, you will need to keep an open mind while you're checking the news for the reason behind a price movement. Indicators are used to detect chart events, such as whether or not the price is trending, how strongly it is moving, and whether or not a trend turning point has been achieved. The goal of indicators is to clarify and enhance your impression of price movement by providing you with more information and tools. Indicators are categorized into two categories, and they are the judgment based indicators and the mass based indicators.

Visual pattern recognition methods such as bar line and pattern analysis, as well as candlesticks are included in what we call that judgment based indicators. Indicators like this might take a lot of effort to learn how to utilize and understand. This means that you can't back test them to see how they would have performed across the price history of your security. On the other hand, moving averages, regressions, momentum and other forms of computations are what is in the math based indicator group. Calculating chart events mathematically allows you to assess how effectively to anticipate future price movements due to the fact that they are quicker, cleaner and more so-called scientific.

People are often more likely to utilize math based indications. Now, truth be told, both present price data in a specified manner to help you make a trading choice. Although mass based indicators are fond of mathematics, they are nonetheless still pretty much subjective like this. Judgment based indicators are thus techniques based on judgment, and those based on math are both legitimate and beneficial, but both are subjective. Some traders rely solely on visual identification techniques, while others rely solely on mathematical indications. Now, don't worry if math isn't your thing. Mathematics isn't tough in most technical analysis because the indicator identifies a crowd's behavior.

You don't really need to know the math behind it to use it. And also with both of these indicators, I'm not going to teach you how to get those and read those, because what I will provide you is free tools that you even need to sign up. That does all of the hard work for you. So basically, you only need to know what those are, essentially, and they will do the hard work for you for free. Now, there are three main trend directions that technical indicators have, and they are when a trend just started or when they could also review whether the trend is as strong or weak or just trading sideways, as well as they could also indicate when there is a trend of reversal.

Now, some indicators perform better than others in certain situations. And as a result, if you asked 10 technical traders to name their best indication for each assignment, you probably get completely different lists of indicators from each one of them. Heck, if you ask, given millions of technical traders, you will probably find a lot of distinct patterns among them, too. Ideally, you would first establish a stock that you're analyzing is trading or range trading sideways and then apply the relevant indication to a trading strategy accordingly.

You can't always categorize price movements as trending or on trend trending. And aside from that, prices typically have a range, whether they're trending or not. That can be identified. A trader's own trading strategy usually falls into one of two categories, and they are the trend followers and the swing traders. The first type are the trend followers, and the strategy involves waiting for retracement and trading ranges to settle back into a more obvious trend. And as a result, some trend followers utilize information from momentum indicators to alter their positions, such as taking a profit when the asset becomes over, Baatar oversold, even when the trend is only pausing to anticipate it to go on for a long time to come.

Swing traders, on the other hand, involve mostly buying low and selling high. While trend following is more rigid, swing trading is more flexible since it may be used in a variety of market circumstances. But the downside of swing trading is that it necessitates more frequent trading, and each leg of the deal tends to provide lesser profits than a single trend following trade. Those who choose trend following must endure the downturn in an upward trend or the upward bounce in a downtrend. The trend will resume if you have correctly detected it. On the other hand, choose a strange swing. Trading requires a certain amount of bravery, since you may be trading against the trend at times.

Always keep in mind that your choice of trending or swing trading indicators influences the length of your holding period. When using trending indicators, it is more likely to keep you in a trade for longer than when using swing trading indicators. There's a lot of strength in simple old fashioned approaches, like a bar reading and pattern detection. And the same is true for math based indicators. But if you discover that you can't convey market sentiment or what the public is experiencing from a math based indicator, don't bother using one. It is important to keep in mind that just one indicator based rule may make or break you. Such as purchasing when your stock picks a resistance line or selling when it goes below a moving average.

Typically, the price and volume changes are measured in relation to prior prices and volumes during particular lookback periods, such as 12 or 21 days. Studies have shown that most indicators function best within a certain timeframe. In most charting applications, you may find pre formatted indicators with default parameters, such as the momentum indicators that I'm going to touch based on later has a 12 period cycle. This is only a starting point. And if 12 peers doesn't work as a momentum indicator for you, feel free to use a different amount of periods in your momentum indicator. Code 12 12. Period was just historically determined to be the most optimal number. Doesn't mean that it applies to you, though, because prices are so fractal and indication may apply to any time range.

For example, daily bars are like microcosms of intraday bars and weekly or monthly bars or like microcosms of daily bars. Any time price changes occur. Traders will react in a similar manners note. You should remove the notion of knowing your time period before choosing indicators, depending on how you interpret the indication. It may be more flexible than you previously believed. For example, to trade long term, you can utilize indications that are short term. There are AIMA short term. Thousands of technical traders across the world are actually always coming up with new ways to use indicators almost daily or monthly. So be sure to explore what is best for you and develop a set of tools and analysis methods that are more match to your investment pattern.

Of course, signals are probably the most important part of technical analysis because it provides indications of when to buy and sell stocks. However, in many cases, the signal is more like a warning, and that does not have a black and white decision rule containing it. Indicators create signals in three different ways, and they are the crossovers. The price range limits and the conversions and diversions. Now, when a line crosses another, this is called a crossover trading and technical analysis. Crossovers happen when a fixed historic benchmark is crossed or a price crossing. The indication or the indicator crossing the price or an indicator's first line crosses the second indicator line.

One of the most significant ideas in technical analysis is when the price crosses an indication where sometimes this phenomenon is called what we called a precut. So when a price climbs over a long standing resistance line, technical traders say it broke out of its previous trading range and now the sky's the limit until the new range is set. Most of the time, you will want to watch and measure up breakout with care. The very phrase Preko tells you a lot about the psychology of the audience that's driving the price surge. Now, a breakup doesn't always mean a trend reversal. It can also be a sign that an established trend is gaining pace or crossing new milestones as well. Next, let us talk about price range limits under this category.

We have something called an oscillator that describes the price relative to their trading range. Oscillators run from zero to one hundred or negative one hundred to one hundred or any other variant utilizing the number of one hundred. As a result, traders draw a line at 20 percent of a maximum price range and another at 80 percent of the maximum price range in order to ensure that the price range does not exceed the outer boundaries, or 10 percent and 90 percent or some other variation. This means that when an indicator gets close to a line, it's indicating the price is getting close to a recent high. And overbought or oversold state is being signaled in this case indicating a probable pullback or reversal.

Lastly, we have the convergence and that divergence, a convergence occurs when two indicator lines get closer together, such as one to support line and resistance line form a triangle or in two, moving averages grow closer together, suggesting less of a difference between their numerical values, respectively. As a result of convergence, the price action tends to go laterally or has a tighter range of highs and lows. It is common for breakout to follow a sideways move and vice versa. Despite the lack of a built in trading rule, convergence is more typically employed as a signal that a trend is shifting direction or strength.

On the other hand, indicator lines that are moving farther apart, such as the spread between two moving averages, are considered what we call divergent, an indication that the price diverging is also known as what we call divergence. And when it comes to momentum indicators in particular, they shuffle the price pass components in order to arrive at a price rate of change, resulting in a complex estimate of the trends of strength. A divergence occurs when the price continues to rise or making new highs while the momentum indicator begins to decline or making progressively lower highs, despite the fact that, like convergence, divergence does not come with an inherent trading rule. But it is nevertheless worth noting as a signal of a future trend change.

Now, I have mentioned previously quite a few times about something called momentum. So now let us talk about momentum. Momentum is the term coined from physics, where it describes the strength of a moving object's speed. Although many momentum indicators do not utilize the word momentum in their titles, momentum is still a general concept that covers a wide range of technical indicators in this situation as well in technical analysis. The worst momentum and rate of change are pretty much interchangeable in general. Momentum indicators may be used to produce, buy, sell signals or to assess, buy, sell signals provided by other indicators, depending on the application.

Unlike trend following indicators such as moving averages, momentum acts as a leading indicator and may be utilized to overcome the lag during a sideways market. Momentum indicators Excel are predicting an approaching shift. In addition, some momentum measures are key to identify whether an asset is overbought or oversold on a chart. Your eye naturally attempts to line up a momentum indicator with the price movement. If you look at the direction of the price indicator, it's likely that you will assume you're seeing a link between that and the momentum indicator. Oftentimes, you're not really wrong. But however, it may also be misleading. The computational momentum shows the speed. It is easy to believe that momentum has slowed down when your momentum indicator online is horizontal.

But this isn't the case at all. It actually means we've come to a halt and acceleration. So the pricing momentum might be pointing to somewhat similar directions. It means something completely different. Despite the fact that momentum is not a trend indicator, like a moving average, it does tend to reflect trends. Now, why is this so? Well, this is because human beings and their emotions are at the root of price movements. Investors jump on the bandwagon as the price starts to rise, causing it to rise at an even quicker pace. Hence, it is not unexpected that the slope of the price moves steepens at the same time as the momentum in indicator's slope. Even if traders are adding to their holdings, the market may still close higher than it did at the start of the rise. Despite the slowdown in the trend, you're going to still be making money.

Lastly, for technical analysis, I want to touch base on the concept of volatility. Now, volatility is a measure of price variation. Either the overall movement from a central measure such as average or the volatility between low and high during a given period of time, there is direct correlation between the volatility and the risk. If volatility changes, the predicted price range will also be very volatile. Securities have a broad range of probable outcomes, and therefore they're difficult to predict. Likewise, a non-volatile security has a limited and thus more predictable range of possible outcomes compared to the volatile ones. In order to modify your profit goals and stop loss to reflect the changing chance of gain or loss, you must keep a close eye on volatility as a standalone metric or indication.

Variance is not used by traders and is not included in many software charting packages. Now, why is that? What for the same reason as a standard deviation variance is not immediately usable as a standalone metric. But variance is pretty much what is behind the concept of a volatility indicator. Now, everything revolves around time, and depending on the time range you're looking at, your perception of volatility will change. Now, why are there so many contradictory generalizations regarding volatility? Well, you can tell a lot about a trader by the time over which they measured. The volatility indicators are important, but so is the way you view risk.

Although two traders may be using the same indicators, they may have different results because they handle the trade differently by looking at volatility differently, such as scaling in and out, choosing a stop loss level and so on. Sometimes volatility may be thought of in terms of crowd sentiments when traders become enthused about a fresh move. Volatility increases to a new high or low as expected, which causes bullish traders to take up fresh positions and bearish traders to scurry to get out of the way. Get out of the way as stock losses cascade. When you have higher highs and the lower those you are starting, a new move is very uncommon for volatility to be extremely low.

Just before turning point and excessively high just before a new trend takes off. However, the unpleasant reality of trading is that volatility may be high or low for no apparent price related cost at times. In contrast, low volatility indicates less immediate danger. A little bit of volatility isn't always a good or a bad thing when volatility is stable. You can estimate the maximum possible gains and losses with more position volatility. Norms vary from security to security as fundamentals and trading populations shift. Is possible to give a security a personality based on the aggregate risk appetite of its traders. So depending on your own appetite of risk, your view of and use of volatility indicators may be different.

Derivatives

In this video, I'm going to touch on the topic of derivatives. Let us start off with what is a derivative, a derivative is a financial instrument whose value is derived from the value of another asset, which is referred to as the underlying. Assuming that you've signed a legal contract that offers you the option to acquire a fixed quantity of silver at a predetermined price of ninety dollars at any time in the next three months in exchange for a premium on the global market. Silver is presently valued at eighty dollars. The underlying is silver. And the other option in this case is what we call the derivative.

If the price of silver rises, the options value rises as well, because it provides you the right, but not the responsibility to buy the metal at a certain price. Now, assume that the market price of silver increased dramatically in the weeks after the contract signage and the quantity mentioned in the contract was now worth one hundred and eighty dollars. Then if you want to exercise or take out the option, you could buy the silver for ninety dollars and sell it to a dealer for one hundred and eighty. The option contract now has grown in value over time. Assume instead that the price of silver has plummeted and the contract quantity stated is only worth fifty dollars.

The contract would then be practically meaningless, and it is unlikely to ever be used. Derivatives can be based on a large number of different underlying assets metals like gold and silver. Commodities like wheat and cotton. Energy resources like oil and gas and financial assets like stocks, bonds and foreign currencies are all examples of this in every situation. There is a value correlation between the derivative and the underlying commodity or financial asset. For example, an option to buy a share at a fixed price is a derivative of the underlying stock, since the options value rises in tandem with the stock's price in a derivative transaction. The amount at risk is generally, but not always significantly less than a nominal value.

Users can have exposures that are almost comparable to those in the cash market, such as changes in foreign exchange rates, interest rates or stock indices. But with little or no exposure to the principal or nominal value, thanks to the usage of derivatives, because the risk associated with derivatives is smaller than that associated with cash instruments, the amount of capital necessary to be set aside by banks. Trading derivatives is far lower than that required by banks trading cash. This, together with its flexibility and liquidity, is a major reason for the appeal of derivatives. There is a vast array of derivative instruments available today.

These are exchanged on established exchanges directly agreed upon in a so-called over-the-counter or OTC market where trades are made over the Internet or traditional Letho phone they're categorized in for simple groups, which are forwards futures swaps and options. Let's go over what each of these are. Let us start with forwards. A forward contract is a contract between two parties that is made directly between them. One party promises to acquire a commodity or financial assets at a specified price on a future date. The other party agrees to supply the commodity or asset at a specified price.

The agreement contains no element of flexibility regardless of the value of the commodity or asset at the time of delivery. Both parties are obligated to complete the contract, which is a legal and enforceable obligation. The terms and circumstances of a contract can be modified since they're negotiated directly between two parties. However, there's a chance that one party will fail to meet its commitments. The next one is called futures. A future contract is similar to a forward contract, except that instead of being negotiated directly between two parties, the agreement is constructed through an organized and controlled exchange.

One party promises to provide a commodity or asset on a defined range at a future date or a range of dates, and the other party agrees to a set delivery. The contract is a legally enforceable agreement forwards and futures defers in three important ways. To begin with, a future contract is protected against default. Second way is that future contracts are standardized to encourage aggressive trading. And the third way is that they're settled on a daily basis. The third type is called swaps, a swap is a contract between two parties to exchange payments on a regular basis in the future of the payment lakes completed differently because swaps are otc transactions. There is a chance that one or both parties will default on their commitments.

Swaps are used to control or hedge the risk associated with interest rate, currency exchange, commodity and stock market volatility. A common scenario is when a firm borrows money from a bank at a variable rate and is upset about two interest rate increases. By entering into a swap, the company may lock in its financing costs. The last category is options. Options are derivative financial products dependent on the value of underlying securities like stocks. An option contract gives the buyer the choice to purchase or sell the underlying asset, depending on the contract type. Unlike futures, the holder of an option is not obligated to buy or sell the asset if they do not choose to.

There are two main types of options. Mainly call and put a call option offers the holder the right to purchase an underlying asset at a specified price by a particular date. A put option, on the other hand, gives you the right to sell an underlying asset at a specified date, in particular at a specified price by a particular date. The buyer of an option must pay the seller or write off the contract an initial sum of money known as the premium. This is due to the options. Flexibility is never required to be used. So that is why you need to pay a premium. Options are either freely traded on established exchanges or negotiated between two parties in the market, one of whom is usually a specialized dealer. Generally traded options are standardized goods.

Now, we will go through some of these in more detail later on in this video. Let us now go over the players in the derivative market, dealers, hedgers, speculators and arbitrageurs are the four primary participants in the derivative market in various market situations. The same persons and organizations may play different roles. A vast number of people and organizations are also helping the industry in various ways. So now let's go through each one of these. The first is the dealer dealers who work for big banks and security firms buy and sell derivative contracts. Some contracts are exchanged on exchanges while others are treated over the counter. The derivative business of a big investment bank is today a highly specialized activity center.

The traders who handle the banks to manage any risk that the bank faces as a result of delivering customized products for clients. The second type are what we call hedgers. Derivative products are used by corporations, investment institutions, banks and governments to hedge or minimize their exposure to market factors, including interest rates. Stock prices, bond prices. Currency exchange rates and commodity prices. The farmer who buys futures contracts to lock in a price for delivering a crop at a later date is a famous example of hedging a buyer in this case, maybe a food processing firm or a speculator who wants to lock in a price for taking delivery of the crop in the future.

Another common scenario is a firm that expects to receive a payment and a foreign currency at some point in the future. It agrees to sell the foreign currency and receive a preset amount of local currency in a transactional bank. Alternatively, you can purchase an option that provides at the right, but not a responsibility to sell foreign currency at a certain rate. Another type of participants are called speculators. Derivatives are ideal for trading, commodity and financial asset prices, as well as important market factors, including interest rates to market indexes and currency exchange rates in general. Utilizing derivatives to establish a speculative position is significantly less expensive than treating the underlying commodity or asset.

As a result, the prospect of profits are significantly higher. The trader who believes that increased demand or lower output and has the market price of a commodity is a typical example of a speculator. The last type of participants are the arbitrageurs, and the arbitrage is a transaction that generates a risk free gain by taking advantage of a market mispricing. A basic example is when a trader may buy an object for a low price in one place while concurrently arrange to sell it for a greater price in another, arbitrageurs would rush in to acquire the asset in the cheap location. Narrowing the pricing gap, such changes are unlikely to last long. Arbitrage possibilities often occur in the derivative sector, since a product may be built in a variety of ways, using various building pieces.

If a product can be sold for more than it cost to acquire the individual components, a risk free profit may be made. However, the presence of transaction costs typically implies that such possibilities are only available to Pakenham market actors. So now let us talk more about forewords, a forward contract is an agreement established directly between two parties to purchase and sell a commodity or financial asset at a predetermined price on a certain day in the future that is agreed upon at the beginning. Forwards are over the counter bilateral transactions in which at least one of the two parties is a bank or other financial institution, corporations, dealers and investment organizations who are searching for deals that are suitable for their unique needs.

Employee and transaction futures are standardized contracts exchanged on organized and controlled markets that have comparable economic consequences. Forwards have counterparty risk, which is the possibility that the other party to the transaction may fail to meet its contractual commitments. A senior trader contracts today to acquire a share at an asset price of fifty dollars in a year's time. This is an example of a long position or a purchase of a stock. Now, if that share is worth ninety dollars in a year, the trader can acquire it through a Ford contract and sell immediately for a profit of forty dollars. If, however, the share is only worth twenty dollars after a year, the trader is still required to purchase it for fifty dollars.

And in that case, the loss is 30. If we now look at the counterparty or the other party to the deal, they have agreed to sell the share to the trader for a predetermined price of fifty dollars in a year's time. Now, this is a short forward position, also known as a forward sale. If the share is selling for less than fifty dollars at the time of delivery, the counterparty will profit from the transaction, since he or she can acquire it for less than fifty dollars and then deliver it via the forward contract for exactly fifty dollars. On the other hand, the counterparty will lose money on the Ford contract if the share is valued at more than fifty dollars in a year's time.

Now, a forward contract is an agreement between two parties to purchase and sell an item at a specified price at a future date. And this raised the question of how they will ever agree on a fair or reasonable price for delivery at some point in the future. Well, a cash and carry calculation, as it is known in the derivative industry, provides this answer. This technique is founded on the idea that in an active and efficient market, arbitrage possibilities should not exist. An arbitrage is a series of transactions that result in risk free profits due to market mispricing of assets. This sort of opportunity is referred to by some traders as a free lunch. Now, let's pretend that a stock is trading at six dollars in a cash market, which is the market for buying and selling securities for immediate delivery.

A client then contacts us with the request to purchase the stock at a preset price in exactly one year. Now, how can we arrive at a reasonable price for this forward contract by contacting a sample of research, analog or reviewing charts of his previous price performance and projecting future movements? We could determine the level at which the shares most likely to be traded at the moment of delivery. Those are issues that everything is very hypothetical. And if we make a mistake and set the floor price or the price at which we will sell the client share after a year too low, the contract might lose a lot of money.

So now is there a method to determine a reasonable forward contracting pricing without having to incur this risk? Well, we can borrow six dollars and purchase the stock and the cash or spot market, then keep carrying it for a year until it is ready to be delivered to our customer. Assume that the one year interest rate is five percent per annum and that the stock is projected to pay a 20 cent dividend in the coming year. We will have to return six dollars borrowed at a 30 cent interest in a year. But the funding will somewhat be offset by the ten dollar ten cent dividend. So therefore, the formula would be six plus point three minus point one. So that equates to six point two.

This means that the resulting net cash flow in carrying the share generates a negative six dollars and 20 cents a year. And as a result, we will have to charge the customer at least six dollars and twenty cents to deliver the sheriff to the four contracts merely to break even on the transaction. And as a result, a carrot. Cash and carry competition yields six 20, as is that fair or theoretical future price. So now let us go over the components of the forward price in example that we just went through. We estimate a theoretical price of 620, which includes the cost of buying a stock on the open market and a net cost of carrying it for delivery to a customer in a year.

This is what we call the break, even for a price. And for this, the financing fee, which is the interest paid, is subtracted from the dividends received on the share to arrive at the carry cost. Selling forward contracts above this price is very much a free lunch. However, this type of free lunch would not last very long in the real world. The reason for this is because traders would rush in to sell the stock forward to afford the higher price, such as six fifty in this case, while simultaneously purchasing it in the cash price for six dollars in federal funds. The impact would be to drive the four prices back to a point where the arbitrage opportunity vanishes, or it may also pull up the cash price of the share.

The possibility for arbitrage profits keeps the four prices honest that are at or near the fair value computed by the cash and carry technique. And in this case, which is six dollars and 20 cents. With respect to the stock market, traders will acquire forward contracts and short a stock if the market price is below fair value. Shorting is accomplished in practice by borrowing a share of the promise of returning it to the original Unar owner at a later date. And the shares then sold on the cash market. And profits are placed in a money market to generate interest. Traders buying forward contracts while shorting the underlying will cause a floor price to rise back to its theoretical or fair value.

Before arbitrage becomes feasible, before a price of a financial instrument such as stock or bond might give some amount from the theoretical value determined using a simple cash and carry technique. The cost of the transaction is included in the equation in this case. Brokerage and other fees must be paid when purchasing and keeping a stock or bond, keeping a short position and telling borrowing the asset and paying the lender's fees. So how does the cash and caring approach work with non-financial asset forward contracts or commodities, to be specific? Well, in the case of commodities, which are assets kept primarily for the purpose of consumption, the technique must be used with extreme caution.

The reason for this is because it simply does not apply to some commodities, such as fresh fruits, since storing goods for delivery at a later date is impractical in other circumstances. It is only useful in a restricted number of situations. For example, oil, although the simple cash and carry technique implies that the situation should be the complete opposite. The spot price of oil is sometimes higher than the forward of future price in the market. One argument is that major users are willing to pay a premium for oil on the spot market in order to keep it in stock to assure supply continuity. In this case. The former price of an asset is commonly thought of as the projected future spot price on the delivery date.

To put it another way, the floor price is viewed as a forecast of what the assets price will be in the future based on all available data. At the moment, the forward is agreed upon and subject to later revisions based on new evidence. There is at least one reason to assume this, as it would be feasible to build lucrative trading strategies if future prices were prejudiced or distorted in some way. Assume that the market for prices has a systematic propensity to undervalue real spot prices at future dates. Then a trader who bought forward contracts on a regular basis would make more money on trades than he or she would lose.

In some ways, this appears improbable, but it has been suggested that this phenomenon does exist and the resulting profits serve to attract speculators into the market. In fact, there has been a lot of empirical research done on whether or not forward and future pricing are, in fact, skewed in some manner. But results are still unclear in this case. This has significant consequences if we believe that the four price of an asset equals the predicted spot price on the future delivery date as a forward contract and news delivery. Fresh information will be obtained, causing expectations to shift if the information is random. Some of it will be good news for the underlying assets price, and some will be bad news. There is a potential that the underlying will be above the value predicted when the forward contract was signed.

But there's also a chance that it will be below that value at the time of delivery. If the new information is truly random, we may argue that the spot price has a 50-50 probability of being higher or lower than the predicted value. As a result, the chances of profiting or losing money on a forward contract are around 50-50, and the average payment will be close to zero. As a result, neither party would pay a minimum premium to the other to engage into the forward contract from the beginning, because neither side has an immediate benefit. It is worth noting that the situation with options is entirely different. The buyer of an option pays a premium to the seller because he or she has an initial advantage, which is the right to execute the contract in favorable conditions.

But to let it expire otherwise. Next, I want to talk about swaps, the over the counter alternatives to equities index and single stock futures is what is known as an equity swap, is an agreement between two parties to exchange payments at certain interval intervals over a predetermined length of time. Have at least one payment lake based on the value of a share, a basket of shares or stock market index. For this, a payment is paid in a total return transaction that represents the dividends on the share basket or index. When a business has a block of shares in another company, which is also referred to as a corporate cross holding that it wants to monetize or sell for cash. Equity swap application is exercised.

The other company, on the other hand, wants to keep its economic exposure to share price fluctuations for a while. And this company best sells the shares and enters into an equity swap in which it gets a cash payment in exchange for the shares. Equity swaps are incredibly flexible instruments with a wide range of uses for businesses, banks and institutional investors. They may be modified or personalized to meet the demands of clients because they are over the counter agreements made directly between the two parties. A dealer will usually agree to pay the return on practically any basket of shares if some way of hedging or at least mitigating the transaction's risk can be discovered.

This can be useful for an investor who wants to gain exposure to a basket of foreign stocks, but is limited in his or her ownership options. For a set length of time, a swap dealer will promise to pay the return on the shares, both positive and negative, every month or every three months. The investor will pay a variable or fixed rate of interest on a notional principal in exchange. The transaction can be set up such that all payments are made in a familiar currency like the U.S. dollar or the euro. And the situation is likely that the investor as a foreigner will have to pay tax on a dividend income if he or she really acquired two underlying shares. If this is the case, the investor can either participate in an equity swap transaction with a dealer who is exempt from the tax or recover the tax.

The dealer borrows money to acquire the shares and the dealer gives the investor the whole return on the shares, including gross dividends in a swap transaction. In exchange, the investor pays a funding rate, which the dealer uses to service the loan and profit on a transaction in part. The bank, on the other hand, borrows money to acquire the shares and utilizes the investors interest payment from the swap to help pay off the loans interest. The client agrees to pay the swap deal. Any changes in the value of a share if the share price decreases. The swap dealer will pay the client, and if the share price rises, the client will have to pay the swap dealer. This is the equivalent of a short position in terms of economics. Of course, trading equities index and single stock futures allows you to take long and short positions in stocks.

One disadvantage of futures is that they operate on a daily margin system, which may be quite cumbersome; a fixed number of payments are made weekly, monthly or quarterly with an equity swap. Swaps can also be tailored to fit the specific requirements of quants. But futures, on the other hand, are backed by the clearing house, where swaps are over the counter and are subject to counterparty default risk. Lastly, I want to talk about options. Options are financial products dependent on the value of underlying securities like stocks and options contracts that give the buyer the choice to purchase or sell the underlying asset depending on the contract type.

Unlike futures and the holder of an option is not obligated to buy or sell the asset if they do not choose to, the holder of each option contract will have a set deadline by which they must exercise their option, though options or a financial product that may be used in a variety of ways. These agreements involve a buyer and the seller of the buyer paying an option premium in exchange for the contracts. Right. There is a bullish buyer and a bearish seller for each call option, whereas there is a bearish buyer and bullish seller for each option. The buyer will pay a premium charge for each contract, which generally represents 100 shares of the underlying securities buying.

One option, for example, would cost fifty dollars for a contract premium of five 50 cents per share, which is 50 cents times 100 equals fifty dollars. The striking price or the price for purchasing or selling the asset until the expiration date is what is used to calculate the premium. The expiration date also plays a role in premium pricing. The expiration date that the expiration date on foot products specifies when the option contract must be exercised. Options are bought and sold by traders and investors for a variety of reasons. Option speculation enables a trader to retain a leverage position in an asset and a cheaper cost in purchasing the assets shares.

Investors would utilize options to hedge or minimize the portfolio's risk exposure. Option holders can make money by buying call options or becoming option riders in specific situations. For example, one of the most straightforward methods to invest in oil is two options. The daily trading volume and open interest of an option are the two essential statistics for option traders to keep an eye on in order to make the best investing selections. The word Greeks is used in the options market to characterize the many risk aspects involved in taking an options position, whether in a single option or portfolio of options, because they're frequently connected with Greek symbols. These variables are referred to as Greeks.

Each risk variable is the outcome of a flaw in options, assumption or connection to another underlying variable. Traders analyze options, risk and manage option portfolios using several Greek values, such as Delta Theta, among others. Let us go over some of these metrics. The rate of change between the options price and a one dollar change in the underlying assets price is presented by what we called Delta. To put it another way, this is the options price sensitivity to the underlying delta of a call option ranges from zero to one. Whereas the delta of a put option ranges from zero to negative one theta.

On the other hand, is the rate of change between the option price and time, often known as the time sensitivity or option time decay. All other things being equal. The data tells how much an options price falls as the time to expiry decreases the rate of change between the delta of an option and the price of the underlying asset as presented by another cricks alphabet, which is known as the gamma. The gamma value reflects how much the delta would vary if the underlying securities moved by one dollar. Gamma is used to assess how stable the Delta one option is. Greater gamma values imply that Delta might fluctuate substantially in reaction to even minor changes in the underlying price.

Gamma is created for at the money options and lower for in and out of the money options. And it increases in size as expiry approaches. The further away from the expiry date, the smaller the comma value. And this is because options with longer expirations are less susceptible to delta fluctuations. Gamma values generally increase as expiry approaches. Since price movements have a greater influence on Gummo, the rate of change between the value of an option and the implied volatility of the underlying asset is represented by the Greek alphabet . This is the sensitivity of the option to volatility. The Veiga indicator shows how much an options price changes in response to a one percent change in implied volatility.

And lastly, the rate of change in the value of an option versus a one percent change in the interest rate is represented by row. This is a metric for interest rate sensitivity. A short call is a negative to neutral options trading strategy that profits from the underlying assets, downward price movements and the passage of time also known as the Taylor DKA, a long call is a bullish option trading strategy that only profits from increases in the underlying assets price. The short call option strategy is essentially a bearish to neutral options trading strategy that takes advantage of premium DEKAY volatility declines and underlying asset declines. It is not, however, solely a bearish, neutral approach of mine.

A positive movement in the underlying asset selling cause also works because of the potential limitless or undefined potential losses. So he's associated with short calls. Most option firms demand special clearance to treat this technique. The quantity of purchasing power necessary to use a short co-option strategy is determined by exchange loss. Your ProQuest criteria and a degree of approval in your account for each uncovered call. In a standard margin account, a minimum of 20 percent of the underlying asset is required. Margin requirements for short calls are, Of course, determined by the underlying asset. Stocks of a high level volatility may have higher minimum requirements.

The long call options strategy is a bullish option trading strategy with an unlimited profit potential and a restricted lost potential purchase and call options allow you to take a long position on an underlying asset while limiting your net downside risk. Long call options provide an enticing opportunity to get long exposure in an asset for a fraction of the cost of owning the asset outright. Furthermore, the maximum loss is always limited and is generally lower than purchasing the underlying item together. Creating a lower position with call options frees up a lot of money. Furthermore, because it is to be restricted, downside or premium paid and limitless potential, the risk reward ratio is superior.

This is due to the fact that all options involve leverage and there's a high chance of the options being worthless before they expire. Furthermore, because the calls are cheaper, the further out of money they are, there's automatically more leverage. Many traders who buy calls hope to benefit by selling them before they expire, because the profit potential of a long call is limitless. There's no reason for the trade to be closed. The underlying asset might potentially continue to rise, but this doesn't happen very often or at all. When the value of a losing long composition approaches zero, there's no profit to closing it. This is due to the fact that the maximum loss has already been reached and the value either stays the same or grows.

A put option is a financial contract that provides the buyer the right, but not the duty to sell an underlying instrument, such as stop future contract currency or other asset at a predetermined price at any time until the contract expires. Traders can buy to open or sell to open a put option as output is a pot that has been purchased. To open a shotput is a pot that has been sold to open. The long put option strategy is a bearish options trading strategy that profits from rising volatility and falling underlying asset prices. Buying put options, in addition to speculating, is a typical strategy to protect existing law holdings from steep losses. Unlike many other long options, trading methods to long put option strategy includes a profit cap that is reached when the underlying assets drops to zero.

Long calls, on the other hand, have a theoretical profit potential of infinity. The primary motivation for buying puts in an underlying asset is a concern or speculation that the underlying asset will lose value. Only if the underlying asset depreciates, there's a long payoff. Unlike many other options, the strategy is to pay if nothing occurs. The long put option strategy frequently requires significant moves to be successful. Traders frequently purchase plots to synthetically sell a security for the risk of an unlimited loss. In addition to hedging a long position or whole portfolios, the maximum loss when selling a stock or future short or selling to open is potentially limitless. Along puts maximum loss.

On the other hand, as always, the whole premium paid buying option is therefore an appealing alternative for short buyers, traders who want to restrict their upside risk. A short put option strategy is a bullish, neutral or mildly bearish options trading strategy with two variations, which is either cash secure or naked. When a trader sells cash, secured puts implies that they have enough cash to have the underlying asset placed to them where the trader sells naked puts he or she is trading on a margin since the trader does not have enough money to cover short puts. As a result, naked or uncovered short shorts have a significant level of leverage because of the intrinsic probabilities of options.

The short put option strategy is popular. Options that are far out of the money are more likely to expire. Worthless short puts may be a slightly higher health options trading technique for generating revenue from the state of decay and perhaps acquiring the underlying assets of cheaper prices if they're handled appropriately. The SHOT-PUT option strategy is an intriguing option trading technique that is very popular with professional investors. Shotput should always be closed out when the premium is near zero or less than zero point zero five or five cents, because the SHOT-PUT option strategy has a finite profit.

That is due to the fact that the last five cents or put, even if it is well out of the money, maybe practically until expiration, when there is no premium left DKA, the risk reward of holding a shotput turns negative at some time. It is usually a good idea to close out a shot put when it has achieved its maximum profit. A short considerably over the counter with a limited period to expire. With the sole exception, you may potentially save money on commissions by leaving the short put on. Short puts that are lucrative can be ruled until volatility decreases or the price of the underlying asset rises.

Bonds

The capital markets include bonds and stocks. To borrow money and return it, plus interest to the lender or investor over a period of time is what we call issuing a bond, as well as fixed income products and fixed interest instruments. Bonds are also known as fixed income instruments and a money market. Bonds are generally defined as debt instruments of a maturity date of more than one year. Money market debt is defined as a debt that has a maturity of less than one year. Bonds can be issued in a variety of forms. The conventional or simple vanilla bond is the most frequent type of bond or bond matures. It returns its principal, which is equal to the nominal value of the pond. Plus interest at a predetermined rate of four fixed lengths of time until it is redeemed.

There are many distinct types of bond on a market reflecting the many different types of issuers and the requirements for financing. Investing in some bonds is safer than others, and investors benefit from bonds because they provide a steady stream of current income with a guarantee that the loan will be repaid at maturity. A guaranteed investment is one where the eventual payback is almost certain. Bond holders receive compensation at a higher priority than shareholders if the issuing firm defaults. Bonds provide a lesser risk than shares as an investment. And as a result, yields on bonds are usually always lower over the long term. As a result, we can now take a closer look at some of the essential characteristics of bonds.

Before moving forward, let us go over three definitions, which are the issuer principle and coupon rate when it comes to bonds, the term to maturity refers to how many years the issuer will have to pay back the debt. Maturity refers to a bond's expiration date, which is when the bond issuer will redeem it by paying back to bondholders. The principal of bonds term to maturity is an important factor to consider while constructing the bond structure. It shows the bondholder how long he or she may anticipate receiving coupon payments, as well as the number of years until the principal is fully paid. The yield is also affected by the maturity date. Last but not least, the price of a bond will fluctuate for the Book of its life as market yields fluctuate and as all approaches maturity date.

If other conditions are kept the same, bond prices are more volatile the longer they're maturing. And this is because a change in market rates can cause the price of a bond to rise or fall. Principlist amount that the issue commits to pay back to the bondholder and maturity. And it's usually expressed as a percentage. There are other names for this amount, such as the redemption price or maturity price, as well as par value or face amount. Lastly, the rate at the issue of promises to pay each year is known as the coupon rate. Coupon is a term referred to describe the annual amount of interest payments made.

The coupon amount is determined by multiplying the coupon rate by the bonds principle, except for zero coupon bonds. All bonds pay parodic interest due to the fact that they're offered at a significant discount to the principal value. These bonds allowed Holder to earn income, and it is possible to redeem the bonds for the original face value and then earn interest on that difference between the primary value and the purchase price. Local governments sell bonds to fund capital projects such as roads, schools, hospitals and other infrastructures, businesses, on the other hand, issue bonds to raise money for significant projects and to fund recurrent costs. There are many uses of bonds and therefore has led to several bond types available on the Internet.

Some of the bond types are conventional bonds, government bonds, index linked bonds, zero coupon bonds, corporate bonds and high yield bonds. The conventional bonds are the most prevalent, and they feature a set coupon, a maturity date that cannot be changed or extended. They're also called bulat bonds, straight bonds or vanilla bonds, and they have a wide range of uses. As for the government bonds, they're issued by the government and are some of the lowest risk types of bonds. US Treasury notes are one example of government bonds. The third kind is the index-linked bonds. The coupon redemption payment of an index-linked bond is tied to a defined index. The term zero coupon bond refers to bonds that don't pay any coupon payments at all.

There's only one cash flow from a zero coupon bond or strip, which is the redemption payment. That maturity was considered a payment of one hundred dollars. And the issue price would be at a discount compared to a par value. It is the difference between the issue price, which is two hundred dollars in the redemption price, that is used to calculate the interest earned by the bondholder because there's no coupon payments to be invested over the bonds and life cycle. This offers significant advantages for investors. Zero coupon bonds are issued by both governments and corporations. Then there are corporate bonds. Typically, these bonds are issued by non government companies and they might be traditional bonds or a variant of the same concept, because corporate bonds are not risk free like gilts.

They have different levels of credit risk. As a result, the yield on corporate bonds will vary based on market perception of risk. Lastly, there are high yield bonds. Companies with a credit rating below investment grade issued these bonds, which are sometimes known as junk bonds. A higher level of risk for investors means that the yield on the bond is higher than that of, say, government bonds or investment grade corporations. The vast majority of the time, they're not suitable for individual investors to invest in. Bond warrants are derivative instruments that let the holder to either purchase or sell a certain bond at a given price on certain days or within certain timeframes, look, options, bond warrants allow the holder to purchase or sell a bond, but they're not required to do so.

For example, an investor may purchase a bond warrant in order to protect his or her position by assuring that they can purchase the bond if its price increases beyond the warrants price. To borrow money from public or private investors, a firm will issue bonds to the public or private investors. Physical electronic bonds guarantee a fixed or variable interest or interest rate to the person who acquires them. A company can issue bonds with warrants to entitle a buyer to purchase shares at a specific price, usually within a specified timeframe, when they wish to sell bonds at a lower percentage rate than is typical for firms of similar value or performance rating. They typically used this technique. This implies that the words can be sold or redeemed individually.

The striking price or exercise price is the price at which the warrant holder can purchase shares of stock. Most warrants may be exchanged on financial markets, and some firms offer incentives to bondholders who sell or exercise their warrants before they expire. So a firm may not pay a dividend to a bondholder who has warrants that are still outstanding, like warrants. Convertible bonds also allow a buyer to purchase company shares at a set price in exchange for the bonds. A convertible bondholder uses the bond to acquire shares, while a bond holder with warrants sells the warrants or uses additional cash to do so. As for bonds, call options also provide investors the right to purchase shares at a specific price, and it can be exchanged.

They do not have any underlying value, and so do not provide an investor with any kind of security if their price falls below what they paid for them. In the market, many gilt measures are utilized, simple yield or running yield and redemption, yield or yield to maturity are the only two that I'll be discussing here. Let's start with running yield.

The simple running yield is the easiest way to measure the yield on a bond. And the formula for this is running. Yield equals to see divide by P, multiply by 100, where C is the coupon rate and P is the clean price. So what is the clean price? Well, the clean price is the price of a coupon bond, excluding interest payments to have accumulated during the life of the bond.

Now, for the redemption yield, the return from holding a bond is usually measured in terms of its yield to maturity or what we call the redemption yield. As for calculation, we can only calculate al-Juburi, a four zero coupon bond from which the formula is redemption. Yield equals two times the expected square root of value face divided by value, present minus one. If it's not a zero coupon bond, it means that you need to use a numerical root finding technique instead.

IPO Valuation

If you are thinking about investing in an IPO, it might be difficult to decide whether you should try to squash shares from a broker in advance of the IPO or wait until after the IPO to acquire shares. However, in general, IPO usually outperform the larger markets. New IPOs come out all the time, and many technology, health care and media businesses are looking for investors. And virtually all of them have well honed investment chapters. So how can you make sure your money goes to the right place? Well, investors could use a common technique to be selective and determine if a business has the potential to become the next outlier. One of the most important things that you need to read for IPO valuation is to review the S-1 statement.

Now, this is a Securities and Exchange Commission registration statement that is required before a company may sell securities to the public. When you get familiar with the S-1 statement of a forthcoming public offering, your capacity to make an educated choice instantly improves, 12 legally necessary components are included in the prospectus, which is the initial chapter of the S1 in terms of significance. One thing stands out above the rest, and that is really the company's summary chapter. This chapter provides a detailed overview of the company, including its operational and financial history, as well as information on its products and services, as well as its major markets and rivals.

Therefore, most companies spend a lot of time and effort in this area to give a good sense of the long term potential. A realistic evaluation of any risk must also be included in the summary, as well as the whole S1 document, because the goal is to allow investors to do its due diligence, even though that they're supposed to be addressed in a summary part, they're going to be described in much more detailed in a separate chapter at the end of the S1 statement. Now, No. Two prospectus or the same financial schedules, if executive remuneration, principal shareholders, performance metrics, dilution and use of funds are some of the most important parts that follow the summary and should be reviewed as well, if you want to do your due diligence in looking at the S1 statement.

Now, stock market rumor mills and Internet chatter may inflate excitement to a point where it overwhelms an investor's ability of reasoning and increases their fear of losing out on the new and next greatest stock out in the market. But there's an easy method to get the facts from the fog. Now, there are plenty of firms in different growth phases on the IPO calendar, and it is not uncommon for established firms to go public in order to boost their revenue growth by a few percentage points or to optimize their capital structure through some practice. You are able to summarize an issues business model in only a few lines once you get familiar with the prospectus summary within the S-1 statement, as well as trying to comprehend the market need for the company's products or services.

You should be able to explain not just the company's potential, but also where it may fall short of management's expectation. But this comes through experience as you look at more and more as one statement. One very important thing to note is that understanding the company's lifecycle and its profits potential will be very beneficial to determine how urgently one should act on a specific opportunity. As the argument for an instant investment in a fledgling firm with huge Long-Term profit potential and a large demand for its output may be made if everything else checks up, don't forget that the prospectus summary provides both descriptive information and financial statistics.

That was just you to determine where a business is in its life cycle and how much earning potential it looks to have in the prospectus summary. Use of proceeds is a very interesting chapter in particular. Companies go public for one simple reason, which is to raise money from people like you and me. And when it comes to the utilization of profits, well, the S.E.C. demands that an organization explain what it intends to do with its cash and to get the bottom of an issue. All you have to do is read this chapter and find out the truth at its most basic level, study an IPO.

Isn't that different from studying an existing publicly listed firm when it comes to timing? And the requirement to judge relative urgency to its activities are vastly different from another, though there are few offers each year which are so enticing that you might wish to get in before issue and keep four years of life changing profits. But to avoid the yearly disappointments of the IPO market and to identify real market leaders, a little investigation is necessary, as you will be unstoppably gathered by now. However, if you are less appetite for risk in general, I would just recommend you to stick with the existing companies that are already out in the market rather than looking at the next. The next greatest IPO is going to be coming out.

Market Sentiment

In the financial world, market sentiment is a measure of how investors feel about specific asset or financial markets when assets are exchanged in a certain exchange and the prices fluctuate, it reviews how the market is feeling or what its crowd psychology is. A bullish market is characterized by rising prices, and the opposite is true for bearish markets. Investors characterize the market attitude as either pessimistic or optimistic, depending on their perspective. When the bears are in charge, the stock market drops, stock prices rise, when the bulls are in charge. On the other hand, it is not always the case that the stock market is driven by rational thought. Fundamental value focuses on company performance, whereas market sentiment is on mostly feelings and emotions of the people.

Market sentiment can help some investors make money by discovering stocks that are over or under value for this purpose. They utilize a variety of indicators to select the best stocks to trade. When it comes to the market economy, sentiment indicators are meant to indicate how people feel about it as a result of market psychology. These indicators try to measure sentiment either numerically or visually in order to anticipate how present views and positions may impact future market action. Popular sentiment indicators include the CBOE Volatility Index, or VIX, the high low index, bullish percent index and moving averages. Now it is possible to predict investors future behavior using sentiment indicators which measure how bullish or bearish market participants are.

It's possible for them to respond in a contrarian way when sentiment ratings are exceptionally high or low. For example, strong bearishness from the investment community is frequently a hint to sentiment indicator traders that the market might be about to rise. It is also possible for investors to utilize investment indicators in order to determine whether individuals are overly enthusiastic about the present economic or financial situations. Consumer sentiment indicators like the Michigan Consumer Sentiment Report suggest that pessimism may make firms less willing to stock up on goods because they think that consumers will spend as much as usual. Now, the data can be interpreted in a variety of ways.

A high reading indicates that customers are feeling optimistic despite the high reading. Some believe that it will certainly go down in the future. And on the other hand, if the consumer sentiment index is low, then things are likely to become better. However, sentiment indicators should not be used as a trigger for taking action. But as a tool instead, alongside with fundamental and technical analysis to get better insight of the market, investors' view on a given company or asset may be determined by using what we called stocks sentiment, analysis, sentiment. They sometimes are a good predictor of future price movements. Trading psychology may have a significant impact on a market and can be used as a technique to anticipate future price movements in a particular asset.

News, which is economic, political and industry related and social media, are among the variables that impact stocks sentiment. The stock market volatility, trade volume and corporate earnings are all elements that contribute to stock sentiment. However, when coupled with other techniques, such as technical analysis, a greater knowledge of probable scenarios may achieve stock prices, which may be more volatile during periods of extreme volatility. A certain amount of information and emotions such as bad comments on Twitter or social media and in the news can generate anxiety in the market and drive investors to sell a certain stock or firm in a large number of shares.

Positive news, on the other hand, might raise a stock's price. Overbought or oversold circumstances can be swiftly created by an initial surge of fear or enthusiasm, causing the market to move inexplicably large amounts of money. Perhaps the most famous example is GameStop as a result of a campaign by members in the sub Reddit, Wall Street bets game stocks. Stock price surged from seventeen dollars to over five hundred dollars in around January twenty twenty one. Since then, GameStop has become one of the most traded stocks on Wall Street that month. As a result of the hype and unprecedented, unprecedented amount of retail investors bought the company in a bid to dive into hedge funds, betting against it into significant losses.

Now, several disputes followed as GameStop stock gained global attention and became one of the most discussed topics online in late January. Twenty twenty one. These events were followed by a slew of controversies, including brokerage restrictions on trading the stock and the stock market as a whole being scrutinized by the government. Nevertheless, it shows how powerful sentiments can be for the marketplace now. In the next video, as I reviewed the several powerful tools for you to do your stock analysis, you will actually learn a few powerful tools to do sentiment analysis in particular.

Tools for Capital Market Analysis

In this video, I'm going to go over a list of powerful tools that you can use for capital market analysis. No, I do not receive or did not receive any commissions from any of these sites. And all of these tools are free and require no sign ups whatsoever. These tools are what I use daily for my investment portfolio. I've also provided a document containing the links to the tools in a resource chapter under this video. So let us get started. The first tool that I want to introduce to you is the IPO calendars. Now you will find IPO calendars in most stock exchanges. But I'm only showing you one of them, which is from Nasdaq, just because I really like how they organize things. Now, as you can see, the list of upcoming and price companies, as well as a price, a number of shares it is issuing in the IPO calendar and it is spread within the months, in the years.

So you can actually click on the tabs to see what's coming up in the next few months. Now, if you click on one of the entries within the table, you'll then be greeted with an overview like the one you see in front of you. The profile, too, of information such as the actress of the company, number of employees, etc.. However, that is not really very useful information. So what I think is very useful is look at the top of the screen in which you would see three taps. Now there's an overview, the financial filings and experts now, whereas the experts just show you the name of the people that are doing the underwriter, et cetera. The one that I wanted you to look at is the financials and filings.

When you click on it, you can see a very simple table of financials from the company, as well as their filing documents, such as the S1 statement that have just been talked about in the previous video. The IPO calendars are a very good tool in knowing what IPOs are upcoming and contain all the documents that you need in order to do your due diligence in finding out the best company for you to put your money in. Now, the second tool that I want to introduce to you is called the Sea and Dash, which is also known as the capital momentum dashboard. Now, the CRM dash is a very, very good and powerful tool for analyzing overall momentum trends around the world.

And as you can see, there are various categories that you can choose from, such as commodity bonds and node's cryptocurrency currency in general, as well as the various world stock indices. So, for example, if I click under the category of commodity and then click on gold, what it does is that it will pop up the following information in front of you. So now you've got the pricing list like the graph, which you've got the higher low and the close price. But that is not what we want. What we want is that momentum table that's right below. This is what makes the dash so powerful. As you can see, it not only provides you what kind of momentum signals it detects, such as oversold or a buy signal.

It also informs you which particular indicator in which it detects it from. I find this tool extremely powerful because I haven't seen any other tool, which provides you so much detail on momentum in such an effective, efficient manner. If only they allow you to get data from any ticker, that will be even more perfect. But, you know, nonetheless there are very good tech macro trends of the market as well as I mean, it's a free tool. So, I mean, if I'm not paying, I couldn't really complain that much. Now, the third tool that I want to introduce to you is to stock start a comment at a.

Now, after the GameStop situation that happened in the beginning of twenty twenty one people became very interested in monitoring Reddit for sentimental analysis, especially from the sub Reddit, Wall Street bets from which that is where the whole the whole thing stock comments. I really was born from, as you can see from the trending tab, you have the list of most talked about stock tickers and some Reddit as well, whether if the comments are positive or negative. And under the sentiment tab, you will also have the monitoring comments from Wall Street, that's to classify it as a bullish or bearish comment. Now, similarly to Kamdesh, it doesn't really allow you to filter a specific ticker to get your information.

And there is a lot of noise, particularly in this particular tool, just because of how many comments there are and how active Wall Street is in general. However, it is a very good tool for market sentiment. And hey, again, it is a free tool. Now, the fourth tool that I want to talk about is the bull boards from Stock House. Now, this is essentially a forum for which people post a comment and opinion of a given stock. And you can filter it by sector as well as with filtering into any particular ticker. Even some penny stocks will even have their own billboards. And people are actively posting even on penny stock billboards as well. So this place is very good for sentimental analysis. Now, however, though, again, with sentimental analysis, there is a lot of noise.

And in these kinds of billboards, sometimes there are some investors and quite possibly even the CEOs or executives of some of those companies might post here just to gain some noise for their company. So you need to be able to dissect and to analyze yourself whether those comments are actually real or just noise created by people that have a hidden agenda. The fifth tool that I want to show you is stuck to. And this site allows you to do technical analysis really fast. So we just need to type in the trigger in the box below the word home and stock TOCOM and click go. And it will provide you with a very, very in-depth technical analysis report.

As you can see in front of you, it provides you with the various resistance and support it detects, as well as whether it is bearish or bullish in a different time span. So if you are into technical analysis, this is the free tool that you need. The six tools that I want to talk about are Fin DISCOM. Now, this is a financial visualization tool which provides you with a nice heat map of the key winners and losers within the market. So it is very good for screening in general. But I mean, there are a lot of screeners on the Internet, right? You've got Google screener. You've got Yahoo! Finance screeners. So what mix find this so powerful. Why did I choose that? Well, you know what? To be honest, I'm not really much of a fan of heatmap.

So why did I choose fitness? Well, the thing is, if you click on any of the tickers or search any of the particular tickets, it actually provides you with all the fundamental analysis ratios calculated for you. So this is a free tool, not for its free heat map or visualization like it's claiming, but actually it provides all of the fundamental analysis that you need. So this is your tool for fundamental analysis of any particular stock. So the last tool that I want to talk about is Cartmill. Now, at first glance, you might think that it gives you very similar information as finiteness as it provides you with visualization on the market. But, you know, again, within this, I'm not too fond of visualization in general.

So what I really want to tell you is the information that they provide and specifically insider trading. Now, if you click on the top menu on the homepage, you could see a tab of insider trading. And here, it reviews a lot about the list of people who are trading that are in the leadership group within the companies. And this reveals a lot about the company as leadership confidence in or would actually lead to them, whether or not they would want to sell their shares or buy their shares of their own company. But I mean, that tab only gives you the insider trading list of almost all companies so that it's not very useful.

But what you do is you type in the ticker that you want, such as AP1, this case in which what I did in here, you could get a lot of details, such as the the the the price range, the candlesticks, the chart meal rating, which gives you valuation and profitability, etcetera, etcetera. But you also would see a lot of other tabs as well, like technical analysis and fundamental analysis. Well, those two tabs you need to ignore, because those are only for registered users. And I mean, in this video, I'm going for things in which you don't need to do any sign ups. Right. So we already have tools for technical analysis and fundamental analysis. We have already taken care of that.

So here what I want to show you is instead, the ownership to the ownership tab is where you could actually see the dates and the list of names and and the actual insider trading that it happens with every specific company. It also shows you the ownership graph of that company. So an apple in the sense you can look at the pie chart to your left to see how the apple ownership is like. Now, there you have it, the seven free rituals, the covers from finding IPOs to analyzing user momentum, technical and fundamental analysis, as well as deep dive into looking at insider trading.

So these should be more than enough for you to get what you need to analyze any stock. And remember, the list is in a document in the resource chapter of this video. So if you're interested in any of these tools, and I know you are, check out that document or, you know, just keep on pausing on each of the tools in which I introduce to you, because they already have the site. You could just copy that site into your browser and see the magic happen.

Conclusion

Congratulations for you have completed successfully this Book, you have now have the fundamental knowledge of capital markets. You have also learned the basics of fundamental technical and sentimental analysis. You have also learned what derivatives and bonds are as well as now you have a list of three powerful tools in your arsenal to do all of your investment analysis needs. So what are your next steps? Well, your next step should be to start applying these concepts. I would recommend you to go over the list of tools that I've provided you and evaluate your portfolio and make sure that you apply what you learn from this Book into your everyday investment needs.

And I hope that this Book will maximize your investment portfolio. Now, also, if you're interested in the energy industry and the electrical engineering industry, I would recommend you to go visit my other Books. I have Books that are aimed at electrical engineering, especially in the energy industry, the utility industry and the renewable energy industry. Thank you for reading this Book. I hope to see you in my next Book.

Don't miss out!

Visit the website below and you can sign up to receive emails whenever ADIL KHAN publishes a new book. There's no charge and no obligation.

https://books2read.com/r/B-A-GZFBB-KYDYC

BOOKS 2 READ

Connecting independent readers to independent writers.

Also by ADIL KHAN

Business Strategy Understand What It Takes To Be Successful In Business
Emotional Intelligence Gaining Control Over Emotions
Project Management - Complete Guide For A+ Project Managers
Accounting 101 Learn The Basic Principles The Right Way
Influencer Marketing Launch Powerful Campaigns In 10 Steps
Sales Skills Mastery: Sales Story & Metaphor Techniques
Proven Manifestation, Law Of Attraction Self Hypnosis System
Forensic Accounting, Fraud Investigation And Fraud Analytics

www.ingramcontent.com/pod-product-compliance
Lightning Source LLC
LaVergne TN
LVHW022209200926
848481LV00006B/1899
9798224915590